Defoe Abbott Marx Hardy Machiavelli Montaigne Chesterton Cooper Emerson Joyce Austen Hugo Eliot Grimm

Melville Carroll Christie Haggard Molière

Stoker Wilde Maupassant Byron Schiller Kafka

Garnett Einstein Fitzgerald Engels Smith Hall

Goethe Hawthorne Willis

Cotton Dostoyevsky

Baum Henry Kipling Doyle

Leslie Dumas Flaubert Turgenev Nietzsche Balzac Crane

Stockton Vatsyayana Verne

Burroughs Whitman Gogol Vinci

Curtis Tocqueville Busch

Homer Widger Tolstoy Twain Scott Plato

Darwin Thoreau Harte

Potter Freud Zola Lawrence Dickens Burton Hesse

Kant Jowett Stevenson Cooke

Andersen Cervantes

London Descartes Voltaire

Poe Aristotle Wells

Hale James Hastings Irving

Bunner Shakespeare Cooke

Richter Chekhov Chambers da Shaw Wodehouse

Doré Dante Swift Pushkin Benedict Alcott Newton

tredition was established in 2006 by Sandra Latusseck and Soenke Schulz. Based in Hamburg, Germany, tredition offers publishing solutions to authors and publishing houses, combined with worldwide distribution of printed and digital book content. tredition is uniquely positioned to enable authors and publishing houses to create books on their own terms and without conventional manufacturing risks.

For more information please visit: www.tredition.com

TREDITION CLASSICS

This book is part of the TREDITION CLASSICS series. The creators of this series are united by passion for literature and driven by the intention of making all public domain books available in printed format again - worldwide. Most TREDITION CLASSICS titles have been out of print and off the bookstore shelves for decades. At tredition we believe that a great book never goes out of style and that its value is eternal. Several mostly non-profit literature projects provide content to tredition. To support their good work, tredition donates a portion of the proceeds from each sold copy. As a reader of a TREDITION CLASSICS book, you support our mission to save many of the amazing works of world literature from oblivion. See all available books at www.tredition.com.

Project Gutenberg

The content for this book has been graciously provided by Project Gutenberg. Project Gutenberg is a non-profit organization founded by Michael Hart in 1971 at the University of Illinois. The mission of Project Gutenberg is simple: To encourage the creation and distribution of eBooks. Project Gutenberg is the first and largest collection of public domain eBooks.

Memoirs of General Lafayette

Samuel Lorenzo Knapp

Imprint

This book is part of TREDITION CLASSICS

Author: Samuel Lorenzo Knapp
Cover design: Buchgut, Berlin – Germany

Publisher: tredition GmbH, Hamburg - Germany
ISBN: 978-3-8424-3019-8

www.tredition.com
www.tredition.de

MEMOIRS OF GENERAL LAFAYETTE

WITH AN ACCOUNT

OF HIS

VISIT TO AMERICA,

AND OF HIS RECEPTION BY THE

PEOPLE OF THE UNITED STATES;

FROM HIS ARRIVAL, AUGUST 15TH,

TO THE

CELEBRATION AT YORKTOWN,

OCTOBER 19TH, 1824

by Marie-Joseph-Paul-Yves-Roch-Gilbert du Motier,

MARQUIS DE LAFAYETTE

ADVERTISEMENT,

BY THE EDITOR.

* * * * *

It is a poor apology to offer for any defect or omission in a work intended for the information of the public, that it was prepared in haste. Yet in the present case it can be offered with truth. The Editor of this volume knew nothing of the plan, until it had been some time proposed, and many subscribers obtained. The gentleman by whom it was first intended to have been prepared, was suddenly taken away, without writing, or even collecting any thing for the volume. It was undertaken with reluctance, as it was known the public would he impatient for the work, and as the publisher was also desirous it should be prepared in a few weeks. It is only fifty days since the task was begun. It is believed, however, that several documents, not yet published, will be found in this volume; and that many events and incidents are preserved, which would otherwise have been lost to the public.

Everything relating to the life and character of this extraordinary man, is certainly worthy of remembrance by the benevolent and intelligent through the civilized world, and especially by Americans, to whom he has rendered the most essential services. The endeavour has been to avoid panegyric; though in this case, a plain statement of facts may be construed, by those ignorant of the life of Lafayette, into a disposition to bestow extravagant praise.

It has been a source of much satisfaction to the Editor, to find so many proofs of consistency and of principle, as well as of zeal in the cause of rational liberty, which the life of this heroic and disinterested personage affords. And if he shall appear in this hasty memoir, as the ardent, undeviating, and sincere friend of civil freedom and of the rights of man, it will be because he justly merits such a high character.

In the account of his reception by the people of this country, in various places, during his present visit, it may be thought that we have been too particular. It was promised, however, in the proposals for the volume, that such relation would be given. It is believed that it will be found to be interesting, and that it will be a satisfaction hereafter, to recur to it. This account embraces the time which elapsed after he landed at New-York, August 15, 1824, to the celebration of the capture of the Brittish [sic] army at Yorktown, October 19. These statements were, copied principally from the public newspapers; and it was thought to be unnecessary to give credit for them, or to insert the usual marks of quotation.

Boston, Nov. 1, 1824.

TABLE OF CONTENTS

MEMOIRS

OF

GENERAL LAFAYETTE

* * * * *

Among the many great men who have distinguished themselves in the present age, for their attachment and devotion to the cause of civil liberty, general LAFAYETTE is one of the most eminent. During the last fifty years, great changes have been made or attempted in human governments, highly favourable to political freedom and the rights of mankind. In some cases, indeed, revolutions have not been conducted upon just principles nor by prudent councils; and the immediate results have been disastrous rather than beneficial. Changes have taken place without direct and visible improvement; and efforts to meliorate the condition of man have produced a reaction in the adherents to patient arbitrary systems, which have given occasion to much suffering and great excesses.

The struggle for freedom by the patriotic citizens of America, towards the close of the last century, was successful; and has proved most auspicious to human happiness. We have reason to hope, that its blessings will not be contined to this western continent. A spirit of enquiry, indeed, has gone abroad in the world. It is spreading in Europe: and though we devoutly wish it may not prove the occasion of bloody contests, we shall rejoice to trace its fruits in the gradual destruction of old despotic systems, and in the general diffusion of knowledge among the people, and the enjoyment of those equal and just rights, which mild governments are calculated to secure.

In our own beloved country, we can boast of many sincere patriots and heroes besides our 'paternal chief,' the revered WASHINGTON, "who was first in war, first in peace and first in the hearts of his countrymen;" others will be recollected, who devoted themselves to the cause of liberty and their country, with a sincerity and zeal almost without a parallel in the annals of history. Their memories will not cease to be revered while Americans are distinguished for a love of civil freedom.

It must be acknowledged, however, that there was a *peculiar* disinterestedness in the services and sacrifices of the Marquis LAFAYETTE in defence of American independence. It was from a noble and enthusiastic love of liberty, that he was induced to cherish and advocate our cause. It was for strangers and in a foreign land, that he went forth to defend the rights of man, assailed by the hand of arbitrary power. He was not a desperate adventurer, without fortune, or friends, or honors. He was surrounded with all these in his own country. He belonged to very ancient and noble family, and inherited a large estate. The original family name was Motier; but for several generations back had assumed the addition of *Lafayette*. Some of his male ancestors were distinguished for military, and some of the females for literary talents. His income was 200,000 francs. His property and influence were increased by a matrimonial connexion with a lady of the truly illustrious house of NOAILES. He was married at the age of eighteen.

MARIE-PAUL-JOSEPH-ROCH-YVES-GILBERT-MOTIER DE LAFAYETTE was born at the chateau de Chavagnac in the province of Auvergne, September 6th 1757. The rank and affluence of his family secured for him the best education: and this, according to the fashion of the times in France, was not only in classical and polite literature, but united also a knowledge of military tactics. At the age of sixteen, he was offered an honorable place at Court, which he declined.

His mind was early imbued with an ardent love of freedom. It is not known whether his study of English writers who were friendly to civil liberty, or an eager curiosity to learn the merits of the dispute between Great Britain and the American colonies, lead him first thus to take a deep interest in favour of our independence. That controversy excited the attention of statesmen on the continent of Europe as well as in England. It has been said that he was acquainted with some distinguished English characters in 1776, from whom he learnt the situation of America, and the object of our revolution. In the latter part of this year, he applied to SILAS DEANE, our agent then at Paris, for information, and encouragement in his plan, already adopted, of rendering his personal service to the cause of America. While he was at Paris, (Dec. 1776) with these views, Dr. FRANKLIN arrived. The intelligence, received from him respecting our situation and prospects at that period, was of a nature to discourage any one, who had not cherished the most enthusiastic and resolute purpose to engage in our behalf. Our almost desperate condition seems only to have increased his zeal and devotion to the interests of America. "Hitherto, said he, I have only cherished your cause; I now go to serve it personally." He believed our cause to be just. He considered it the cause of civil liberty; and gloomy as was the prospect, hazardous as was the enterprize, he was determined to support it at the risk of life itself. In his situation, the privations and sacrifices to be made and endured were incalculably great. It is indeed a singular instance of an heroic enterprize for the good of mankind.

We cannot more justly describe his sentiments and views, than by quoting his own language used at a subsequent period, in a letter to the President of the Continental Congress — "The moment I heard of America, I loved her; the moment I knew she was fighting for liberty, I burnt with a desire to bleed for her." The sacrifices he made cannot be so well otherwise estimated as by reflecting that he left an affectionate wife, in whom he was most happy; and who, he was obliged to assure, that he would speedily return, before she would consent to the enterprize.

When LAFAYETTE made known his purpose to embark for America, under all the appalling circumstances of our country, our Envoys were still unable to furnish a passage for him. They had no vessels at command; and they were not then in a situation to purchase one. Loans were the object of their mission; but as yet they had not succeeded in obtaining them. And as the French court had not acknowledged our independence, or openly espoused our cause, it would have been improper for them to furnish a vessel for such purpose. What was then done for America must be effected in secret; and at most, only connived at by the French government. But the ardour of young LAFAYETTE was not to be checked by any such considerations. He took council rather of his feelings, than of that prudence by which ordinary minds are governed. He therefore immediately engaged a vessel at his own charges, and sailed for the United States, where he arrived in the month of January. He landed at Charleston, S.C. and soon entered, as a volunteer, in the American army. Soon after his arrival, he purchased clothing and arms for the troops under General MOULTRIE in that quarter. He also early made an advance to General WASHINGTON of 60,000 francs, for the public service.

For several months, he continued to serve in this capacity. His zeal and services were early appreciated by Congress; and in July, 1777, he was created a Major-General. But he did not, at once, act under that commission. In the battle of Brandywine, in September of the same year, although he distinguished himself by his activity and undaunted bravery, it does not appear that he acted as Major-General. He received a wound in his leg, in this engagement, and his services were highly applauded. He remained in the field till the close of the battle, inspiring the men by his presence and active courage. The wound was severe and required attention; but before it was entirely healed, he joined the army again under WASHINGTON. In November, at the head of some Jersey militia, he attacked a body of 300 Hessians and defeated them. General GREENE was engaged in the same affair, a part of the time; and said of young LAFAYETTE, "that he seemed to search for danger." Soon after this period, he had command of a division in the Continental army; and frequently was appointed the chief officer in separate departments of great importance and responsibility.

General WASHINGTON became greatly attached to him. He was an intelligent judge of character; and was never known to bestow his confidence upon those who were not worthy of it. He was so distinguished by the regard of the Commander in Chief, that it became usual to call him "his adopted son." WASHINGTON loved him for his goodness, and honored him for his bravery and military talents. In the early part of 1778, when it was proposed to make an attack upon Canada, and to endeavor to connect it with the thirteen United States, Gen. LAFAYETTE was appointed to command the troops collecting for that purpose at Albany. This plan originated in Congress, and was said to be much favored by the French Ambassador; but WASHINGTON ever doubted the propriety, or the feasibility of the scheme, and eventually gave his opinion decidedly against it; and it was not prosecuted. It was at this time, probably, that Brigadier General STARK took the oath of fidelity to the American Congress and of renunciation to the king and government of Great Britain, which had then been recently required, before General LAFAYETTE; and which was administered by the commanding officer in each separate Department. The original certificate of this oath is said now to be in existence. It is a singular fact, that a native American took this oath before a foreigner: or perhaps even then, General LAFAYETTE had been declared by Congress to be entitled to all the rights of a citizen of the United States.

In May 1778, while the British main army was in Philadelphia, and the American troops at Valley Forge, he was detached with about two thousand five hundred men under his command, to a position in advance of the continental camp and near the city, for the purpose of watching the motions of the enemy. The British endeavored to surround and surprise him: but he had timely notice of their plan, and retired in safety to the vicinity of WASHINGTON'S head-quarters. Had he been surprised in this situation, the result would probably proved fatal to our cause. For the continental troops under WASHINGTON were few in number and poorly clothed and armed. But the Commander in Chief, doubtless, was fully aware of the important and critical nature of the service, and entrusted it to one, in whose judgment as well as bravery he had perfect confidence.

Soon after this, in the month of June, the British army left Philadelphia, to return to New-York. It consisted of as large a number of well disciplined troops, as they had in America at any one time; and though they chose not to make a direct attack upon WASHINGTON, they seem to have had no apprehensions of an attack from him. But he was resolved to avail of the occasion of their march through the State of New Jersey, to attack and annoy them. This he did on the memorable 28th of June, near Monmouth court-house; and had his judicious plan been faithfully executed, or his own personal activity and bravely been seconded by General LEE, who had the command of the troops more immediately engaged on that day, a great and decisive victory would in all probability have attended the daring enterprize. General LAFAYETTE had a distinguished command on that critical day. Lee, indeed, at first declined the command of the advanced corps, detached by WASHINGTON to harass the rear of the enemy while on their march; and it was given to the former: though; afterwards, when it was found, that the enemy was preparing for a general engagement, a reinforcement was ordered, and the whole placed under the command of General Lee. In this whole affair, General LAFAYETTE conducted with remarkable intelligence and bravery; and received the entire approbation of the Commander in Chief.

In August of the same year (1778) when the enemy had a large force on Rhode Island, and were supposed to be meditating an attack on some place in the vicinity, Lafayette (with General Greene) offered his services as a volunteer. The expedition was not attended with success: the British troops then were more numerous than we could collect against them; and what were mustered were principally militia. The continental regiments were then all needed near New-York. But General Lafayette assisted in conducting the retreat of our men, with much skill and effect; and his behaviour on the occasion received the particular notice and approbation of Congress.

About this time, with the knowledge and consent of Congress, Lafayette made a visit to Boston. The particular object of this journey is not known. It is evident, however, from the resolve of Congress on the occasion, that it was not from merely personal or private views. It was, no doubt, for some purpose of a public nature, and for the welfare of the nation. The following is the resolve alluded to; and is proof, that his visit at the time, was designed for the promotion of some plan calculated for the prosperity of the country.

"In Congress, Sept. 9th, 1778. Resolved, That the President be requested to inform the Marquis de Lafayette, that Congress have a due sense of the sacrifice he made of his personal feelings, in undertaking a journey to Boston with a view of promoting the interests of these States, at a time when an occasion was daily expected of his acquiring glory in the field; and that his gallantry in going a volunteer on Rhode Island, when the greatest part of the army had retreated, and his good conduct in bringing off the pickets and out sentries, deserves particular approbation." This resolve was communicated to Lafayette by the President of Congress, with a polite note; to which the Marquis replied as follows:

"SIR,

"I have received your favour of the 13th instant, acquainting me of the honor Congress has been pleased to confer on me by their most gracious resolve. Whatever pride such approbation may justly give me, I am not less affected by the feeling of gratitude, and that satisfaction of thinking my endeavours were ever looked upon as useful to a cause in which my heart is so deeply interested. Be so good, Sir, as to present to Congress my plain and hearty thanks, with a frank assurance of a candid attachment, the only one worth being offered to the representatives of a free people. The moment I heard of America, I loved her: The moment I knew she was fighting for liberty, I burnt with the desire of bleeding for her: and the moment I shall be able of serving her, in any time, or in any part of the world, will be the happiest of my life. I never so much wished for occasions of deserving those obliging sentiments I am honored with by these States and their representatives, and that so flattering confidence they have been pleased to put in me; which have filled my heart with the warmest acknowledgments and most eternal affection.

"I pray you to accept my thanks for the polite manner in which you have communicated the resolve of Congress; and I have the honor to be, &c.

LAFAYETTE."

During the year 1778, some propositions were made to Congress from the British ministry, through three commissioners, who were sent over to America. The object was to bring about a cessation of hostilities, and peace, without acknowledging our Independence. They were, therefore, immediately rejected. In the address of the commissioners to Congress, the French King and ministers were mentioned with great disrespect, and represented as secret enemies to America; and therefore, not to be believed in their engagements and promises in our favour. The Marquis de Lafayette highly resented this heavy charge against his king and government; and wrote a very spirited letter on the subject, to Lord Carlisle, the principal commissioner. He seemed ready to appear as the champion of his abused Prince and country, in the chivalrous manner such attacks were met in former ages, when disputes were settled between nations by single combat. The indignation he expressed was honorable to his patriotic feelings; but, probably, his maturer years and judgment would have chastened and moderated it.

Early in the year 1779, after an absence from his beloved family and country of more than two years, Lafayette visited France: not however, without the consent of Congress and also of General Washington, and a determination to return to America at a future day. He embarked at Boston. In waiting for a passage to France, the Marquis was several weeks in Boston; and here became acquainted with John Hancock, Dr. Cooper, S. Breck, Esq. and others, to whose families he became particularly attached. The hospitable attention of the Bostonians, was not lost upon him. With warm feelings and elegant manners, he was well qualified to appreciate their patriotism and politeness; and impressions were made upon his generous mind, favourable to their characters, which he has not forgotten to the present day. In no place in America, perhaps, did he find the citizens more congenial to his ardour of affection and devoted love for civil liberty. — It cannot be doubted, that to a man of his amiable and tender feelings, the consideration of meeting with his family and friends influenced him to this visit. But it appears also, from his letters at that time, that he considered his duty to his King and country required him to go to France. War was now declared between France and England; and he believed himself bound to give his personal services for the defence of his own nation. With all his zeal in favour of liberty and of America, which he considered engaged in its sacred cause against an arbitrary power, he acknowledged his obligations to asset in protecting his native country. If his King should consent, he engaged to return to America, and devote himself again in support of her rights. The following letters will justify this statement of his views, at the time of which we are speaking. The first is from General Washington to the President of Congress.

"Head Quarters, Oct. 13th, 1778.

"SIR,

"This will be delivered to you by Major General, the Marquis de Lafayette. The generous motives which first induced him to cross the Atlantic, and enter the army of the united States, are well known to Congress. Reasons equally laudable now engage him to return to France, who, in her present circumstances, claims his services.

"His eagerness to offer his duty to his Prince and country, however great, could not influence him to quit the continent in any stage of an unfinished campaign; he resolved to remain at least till the close of the present; and embraces this moment of suspense, to communicate his wishes to Congress, with a view of having the necessary arrangements made in time; and of being still within reach, should any occasion offer of distinguishing himself in the field.

"The Marquis, at the same time, from a desire of preserving a relation with us, and a hope of having it yet in his power to be useful as an American officer, solicits only a furlough, sufficient for the purposes above mentioned. A reluctance to part with an officer, who unites to all the military fire of youth, an uncommon maturity of judgment, world lead me to prefer his being absent on this footing, if it depended solely on me. I shall always be happy to give such a testimony of his services, as his bravery and good conduct on all occasions entitle him to; and I have no doubt that Congress will add suitable expressions of their sense of his merits, and their regret on account of his departure. I here the honor to be, &c.

"GEO. WASHINGTON."

From the Marquis to Congress.

"Philudelphia. Oct. 8th, 1778.

"Whatever care I should take not to employ the precious instants of Congress in private considerations, I beg leave to lay before them my present circumstances, with that confidence which naturally springs from affection and gratitude. The sentiments which bind me to my country, can never be more properly spoken of, than in presence of men who have done so much for their own. As long as I thought I could dispose of myself, I made it my pride and pleasure to fight under American colours, in defence of a cause which I dare more particularly call *ours*, because I had the good fortune of bleeding for her. Now that France is involved in a war, I am led by a sense of duty as well as by patriotic love to present myself before my king, and know in what manner he judges proper to employ my services. The most agreeable of all will always be such as to serve the common cause among those, whose friendship I had the happiness to obtain, and whose fortune I had the honor to follow in less smiling times. That reason, and others, which I leave to the feelings of Congress, engage me to beg from them, the liberty of going home for the next winter.

"As long as there were any hopes of an active campaign, I did not think of leaving the field. Now that I see a very peaceable and undisturbed moment, I take this opportunity of waiting on Congress. In case my request is granted, I shall so manage my departure, as to be certain before going, the campaign is really over. Enclosed you will receive a letter from his Excellency, General Washington, wherein he expresses his assent to my obtaining leave of absence. I dare flatter myself, that I shall be considered as a soldier on furlough, who most heartily wants to join again his colours, and his most esteemed and beloved fellow soldiers. Should it be thought I can be any way useful to America, when I shall find myself among my countrymen, I hope I shall always be considered as one most interested in the welfare of these United States, and one who has the most perfect affection, regard and confidence for their representatives. With the highest regard, &c.

LAFAYETTE."

"In Congress, Oct. 21. 1778.

"*Resolved*, That the Marquis Lafayette, Major General in the services of the United States, have leave to go to France; and that he return at such time as shall be most convenient to him,—Resolved, That the President write a letter to the Marquis Lafayette, returning him the thanks of Congress for that disinterested zeal which led him to America, and for the services he hath rendered to the United States, by the exertion of his courage and abilities on many signal occasions.

"*Resolved*, That the Minister Plenipotentiary of the United States of America, at the Court of Versailles, be directed to cause an elegant sword, with proper devices to be made and presented in the name of the United States, to the Marquis Lafayette."

The foregoing resolves were communicated to the Marquis in the following letter:

"*Philadelphia, Oct.* 24, 1778.

"SIR,

"I had the honor of presenting to Congress, your letter, soliciting leave of absence: I am directed by them, to express their thanks for your zeal in promoting that just cause in which they are engaged, and for the disinterested services you have rendered to the United States of America.

"In testimony of the high esteem and affection in which you are held by the good people of these States, as well as an acknowledgment of your gallantry and military talents displayed on many signal occasions, their Representatives; in Congress assembled, have ordered an elegant sword to be presented to you, by the American Minister, at the Court of Versailles. Enclosed within the present cover, will he found an act of Congress of the 21st instant, authorizing these declarations, and granting a furlough for your return to France, to be extended at your own pleasure. I pray God to bless and protect you; to conduct you in safety to the presence of your Prince, and to the re-enjoyment of your noble family and friends. I have the honor to be, &c.

"H. LAURENS."

To this note the Marquis made the following reply:

"Philadelphia, Oct. 26, 1778.

"SIR,

"I have received your excellency's obliging letter, enclosing the several resolutions Congress have honored me with, and the leave of absence they have been pleased to grant. Nothing can make me happier, than the reflection, that my services have met with their approbation. The glorious testimonial of confidence and satisfaction respectfully bestowed on me, by the representatives of America, though much superior to my merit, cannot exceed the grateful sentiments they have excited. I consider the noble present offered me in the name of the United States, as the most flattering honor. It is my most fervent desire, soon to employ that sword in their service, against the common enemy of my country and their faithful and beloved allies. That liberty, safety, wealth and concord may ever extend and bless these United States, is the earnest wish of a heart glowing with a devoted zeal and unbounded love for them, and the highest regard, and most sincere affection for their representatives.

"Be pleased, Sir, to present my thanks to them, and to accept yourself the assurance of my respectful attachment.

"LAFAYETTE."

Letter of Dr. Franklin, to the Marquis Lafayette.

"Passy, Aug. 24, 1779.

"SIR,

"The Congress, sensible of your merit towards the United States, but unable adequately to reward it, determined to present you with a sword, as a small mark of their grateful acknowledgments. They directed it to be ornamented with suitable devices. Some of the principal actions of the battles, in which you distinguished yourself by your bravery and good conduct, are therefore represented upon it. These, with a few emblematical figures, all admirably well executed, make its principal value. By the help of the exquisite artists France affords, I find it easy to execute every thing, but *the sense we have of your worth, and our obligations to you.* For this, figures and even words are found insufficient.

"I therefore, only add, that, with the most perfect esteem, I have the honor to be, &c.

"B. FRANKLIN."

The Marquis de Lafayette came again to the United States in April 1780, and landed at Boston, though the vessel first touched at Marblehead on its way to the former place. In his passage both to and from France, he was in danger of capture from the British. The frigate, in which he returned to this country, was chased by an English man of war; and when it was supposed, they must come to action, LAFAYETTE was found at one of the guns, preparing to act his part should they be attacked. In this visit to France, he exerted himself with effect, to induce the Court of Versailles to afford the United States more effectual aid; and especially, to send over a large fleet, which rendered essential service to the American cause. His great devotion to our interests would certainly lead him to advocate any measures with his King, favourable to our wishes: and his influence, considering his high rank and family, was undoubtedly attended with beneficial results. His services in our behalf were particularly noticed by Congress.

"When the Marquis de Lafayette obtained permission to revisit his native country and offer his services to his sovereign, he retained, with his rank in the American army, that ardent zeal for her interests, which the affectionate attentions he had received, the enthusiasm of a soldier in the cause of those for whom he had made his first campaigns and by whom he had been highly distinguished, combined with a consciousness that he was substantially promoting the permanent interests of France; were all so well calculated to inspire in a young and generous mind, in favour of an infant people struggling for liberty and self government, with the hereditary rival of his nation.

"He was received at the Court of Versailles with every mark of favour and distinction; and all the influence he had acquired was employed in impressing on the cabinet the importance and policy of granting sucors to the United States.

"Having succeeded in this favourite object, in which he was aided by the representations of the former and present minister of France at Philadelphia; and finding no probability of active employment on the continent of Europe, he obtained permission to return to America, with the grateful intelligence of the service he had rendered while in France, to the country in whose cause his service had been first drawn. He arrived at Boston in the month of April 1780, and hastened to Head Quarters. He then proceeded to Congress with the information that the King of France had consented to employ a large land and naval armament in the United States, for the ensuing campaign. He was received by WASHINGTON with joy and affection; and by Congress with those marks of distinction and regard to which his *constant* and *indefatigable* zeal in support of the American cause, as well as his signal service, gave him such just pretnesions. The intelligence which he brought gave new impulse both to Congress and to the State Legislatures. The lethargic slumbers into which they seemed to be sinking yielded to resolutions of the most vigorous character." — *Marshall.*

The letters below, with the resolve of Congress, will show the sense WASHINGTON had of the services of his *"adopted son,"* the Marquis Lafayette, and the personal attachment which he cherished for him, as well as the high estimation; in which the disinterested zeal of that devoted friend of liberty was held by the grand Legislature of America.

"Head Quarters, Morristown, May 13, 1780.

"The Marquis Lafayette does me the honor to take charge of this note. I am persuaded Congress will participate in the joy I feel at the return of a gentleman who has so signally distinguished himself in the service of this country; who has given so many and so decided proofs of his attachment to its interests; and who ought to be dear to it by every motive. The *warm friendship* I have for him conspires with considerations of public utility to afford me a double satisfaction in his return. During the time he has been in France he has uniformly manifested the same zeal in our affairs, which animated his conduct while he was among us; and has been, upon all occasions, an essential friend to America. He merits, and I doubt not

Congress will give him every mark of consideration and regard in their power.

"I have the honour to be, &c.

"GEO. WASHINGTON."

To His Excellency the President of Congress."

"Philadelphia, May 16, 1780.

"After so many favors, which, on every occasion and particularly at my obtaining leave of absence, Congress were pleased most graciously to bestow on me, I dare presume myself entitled to impart to them the private feelings, which I now so happily experience.

"In an early epoch in our noble contest, I gloried in the name of an American soldier; and heartily enjoyed the honor I have of serving the United States; my satisfaction is at this long wished-for moment entirely complete, when putting an end to my furlough, I have been able again to join my colours, under which I hope for opportunities of indulging the ardent zeal, the unbounded gratitude, the warm, and I might say, the patriotic love, by which I am forever bound to America.

"I beg you, sir, to present Congress with a new assurance of my profound respect and my grateful and affectionate sentiments.

"I have the honour to be, &c.

"LAFAYETTE"

In Congress, May 16, 1780. "Resolved, That Congress consider the return of the Marquis LAFAYETTE to America, to resume his command in the army, as a fresh proof of the distinguished zeal and deserving attachment which have justly recommended him to the public confidence and applause; and that they receive with pleasure, a tender of further services of so gallant and meritorious an officer."

"Soon after his return to America the Marquis was entrusted with the command of a select corps of the Light Infantry of the continental army. This afforded him a new opportunity for the display of his munificence. He presented each officer of the corps with an elegant sword; and the soldiers were clothed in uniform, principally at his expense. He infused into this corps a spirit of pride and emulation; viewing it as one formed according to his own wishes and worthy of his entire confidence. They were the pride of his heart, and he was the idol of their regard; constantly panting for an opportunity of performing some signal achievement worthy of his and their own character. The corps was probably equal for discipline and bravery, to any in the world."

Early in the year 1781, LAFAYETTE was detached with about twelve hundred troops to Virginia; with a view to co-operate with the French fleet in checking the plundering expedition of General Arnold, who had then recently landed there with a body of British troops from New-York. The Marquis performed this long and difficult march with great dispatch. Many of the soldiers under his command were deficient in clothing: and it was by the personal responsibility of General LAFAYETTE that funds were raised in Baltimore and vicinity to remedy this evil. The credit of the continent was very low; and its means of immediate payment of the public expenses known to be entirely inadequate. The generosity of this distinguished friend of liberty was as remarkable as his personal bravery. He was indeed, both as to life and estate, wholly devoted to the cause of America; and difficulties and dangers served only to manifest the sincerity and intenseness of his zeal in behalf of a people struggling for freedom.

Soon after this, in the month of May, 1781, Lord Cornwallis, in his progress from North Carolina into Virginia, formed a junction with the British forces under Arnold and Phillips. His object was immediately to crush the Americans under LAFAYETTE, then encamped near Richmond. The experienced British Commander thought it would be an easy matter with his superior numbers to secure the "Young Frenchman." But the youthful soldier was not wanting in prudence and foresight, though ardour and courage were his predominant qualities. In these traits of character, as well as others, he was not unlike the "paternal chief" of the American army. LAFA-YETTE made good a retreat; and escaped the net Cornwallis had prepared for him, with such confident hopes of success. He directed his course northward; and soon effected a junction with General Wayne, who had been ordered to reinforce him with eight hundred men of the Pennsylvania line.

The Light Infantry under Lafayette were chiefly eastern troops, who had great objections to a southern climate, and many deserted. In this critical situation, the Marquis adopted the following expedient. He gave out that an expedition of great difficulty and danger was to be soon undertaken; and appealing to the generous feelings of his soldiers, he expressed a hope that they would not forsake him. If, however, any were desirous of returning to their regiments, he said, they should have permission. The effect was as he had hoped. The troops had too much honor and pride to desert their brave commander in such an exigency.

About this time, the main army of the British under Cornwallis, had taken the precaution to cut off the direct communication between the American troops and their stores, lately removed from Richmond to Albemarle. The Marquis Lafayette, however, recrossing the Rappahannock, by forced marches, arrived within a few miles of the British, when they were yet two days march from Albemarle Courthouse; and opening in the night a nearer road, which had been long disused, appeared the following, lay, greatly to the surprise of Cornwallis, between the British army and the continental stores. Thus disappointed in his plan of possessing the American stores, the British commander retired to Williamsburg. The Marquis followed the enemy at a prudent distance; and was soon so fortunate as to form a junction with the Baron Steuben, who had been detached into that quarter, to protect the public stores and assist in the general defence of the country. The British forces, many of which consisted of cavalry, were than very formidable in Virginia.

This was a very critical period in the affairs of America. Washington was satisfied that some decisive blow must be struck; for our finances were low: and many began to despond as to the result of the contest. The British were very powerful and resolute. The plan of Washington finally was to make it appear to the enemy that an attack was intended against New-York; and at the same time prepare for a general expedition to Virginia, and destroy the British army in that quarter. This plan succeeded by the aid of the French fleet, though its Admiral came with reluctance to the measure. Cornwallis and his army were captured in October following; and the British ministry soon after consented to listen to honourable terms of peace.

Major General Lafayette acted a gallant and distinguished part in this whole campaign. We have already witnessed his activity, promptitude and bravery in the early part of the season. His efforts continued, and were conspicuous on various trying occasions. In the affair near Jamestown, he was in great personal danger, and one of his horses was shot under him. It was owing to the to his uncommon vigilance and activity, that the American troops under his command were able to keep a large British army in check; and when a detachment under the brave General Wayne were in danger of being taken, they were rescued by the prompt and skillful maneuvers of the Marquis. His spirit and firmness were attended with the best effects upon the men under his command; and seemed to inspire them with courage and confidence, at this period of great embarrassment and gloom. He was distinguished for humanity as well as courage. The sick and wounded were always sure to receive his generous attentions. In the several engagements which took place, previously to the capture of Lord Cornwallis, many of the American soldiers were wounded, and he made immediate provision for their relief and comfort.

The military skill and bravery manifested by General Lafayette, and the officers and men under his command in Virginia, at this period, will be evident from his letters and orders here given. They speak particularly of the courage and conduct of General Wayne, and his detachment; but they also afford new proofs of the intelligence and activity of the commanding officer.

Letter from General Lafayette, to General Greene.

"Near James River, July 8, 1781.

"SIR,

"On the 4th, the enemy evacuated Williamsburgh, where some stores fell into our hands, and retired to this place, under the cannon of their shipping. The next morning we advanced, and a part of our troops took post about nine miles from the British camp. The 6th, I detached an advanced corps under General Wayne, to reconnoitre the enemy's situation. Their light parties being drawn in, the pickets which lay near their encampment, were gallantly attacked by some riflemen, whose skill was employed to great effect.

"Having learnt that Lord Cornwallis had sent off his heavy baggage under an escort, and posted his army in an open field, fortified by the shipping, I returned to the detachment, which I found generally engaged. A piece of cannon had been attempted by the vanguard, and the whole British army advanced to the wood, occupied by General Wayne. His whole corps did not exceed 800, part of which were militia, with three field pieces. — But at sight of the British, the troops ran to the rencontre, notwithstanding the very superior number of the enemy, and a short skirmish ensued, with a warm, close and well directed fire. But, as both the right and left of the enemy greatly out-flanked ours, I sent orders to General Wayne, to retire to about half a mile, where Col. Vose and Barber's light infantry battalions had arrived, by a most rapid movement, and where I directed them to form. In this position, they remained till some hours in the night. The militia under General Lawson also advanced; but during the night, the enemy retired to the south of the river.

"From all accounts, the enemy's loss is great. We had none killed, but many wounded. Wayne's detachment suffered most. Many horses were killed, which rendered it impossible to move the field pieces. But it is enough for the glory of General Wayne, and the officers and men under his command, to have attacked the whole British army, with only a reconnoitering party, and to have obliged them to retreat over the river. I have the honor to be, &c.

"LAFAYETTE."

Under date of July 11th, an officer of rank gives some further account of this affair. "The enemy had 300 men killed and wounded;

and among the latter were several officers. Their precipitate retreat the same evening, to Jamestown Island, and thence to the other side of the river, is a tacit acknowledgment, that a general action was not their wish. We hear that the British officers are much mortified at the issue, and confess they were out-generalled. Their numbers were far superior to ours; and they had the advantage of a large corps of cavalry. We could not have extricated ourselves from the difficulties we were in, but by the maneuver we adopted; which, though it may have the appearance of temerity, to those unacquainted with the circumstances, was founded upon the truest military principles; and was a necessary, though a very bold and daring measure."

Extract from the general orders of the Marquis Lafayette, July 8th, 1781, near James River.

"The General is happy to acknowledge the spirit of the detachment under General Wayne, in their engagement with the whole of the British army, of which he was an eye witness. He requests General Wayne and the officers and men under his command, to accept his best thanks. The bravery and destructive fire of the riflemen, rendered essential service. The fire of the light infantry checked the enemy's progress round our right flank. The General was much pleased with the conduct of Captain Savage, of the artillery, and is satisfied, that nothing but the loss of horses occasioned that of the two field pieces. The zeal of Colonel Mercer's corps, is fully expressed in the number of horses he had killed."

His conduct at the siege and capture of Cornwallis, at Yorktown, received the particular approbation of the commander in chief. Perhaps no officer in the American line, contributed more than he did to the success which attended our arms on that memorable occasion. When the British General was confident of seizing him and his little party by stratagem, or of overpowering them by numbers, he was on his guard, and had the good fortune to elude every effort to destroy him. And, during the immediate siege of Yorktown, he occupied one of the most dangerous posts, and was among the foremost in the many vigorous assaults made upon the British army, before it was compelled to surrender. He had the honor to be ranked with Lincoln, Greene, Knox, Wayne and others, in the glorious exploits, which convinced the enemy of our persevering bravery, and induced them at last to sue for peace.

In November following, the Marquis returned to France, having first obtained the consent of Congress, and of the commander in chief. The contest between Great Britain and the United States, was drawing to a close. The former became satisfied of the impossibility of subduing America: and the latter was anxious to terminate a war, which had exhausted her finances, and occasioned an oppressive debt. The resolves of Congress, with reference to the departure of General Lafayette at this period, exhibits, in a very favorable light, the important services he had rendered the country, in the critical situation in which it had been placed.

In Congress, Nov. 1781. "Resolved, That Major General Lafayette have permission to go to France, and to return at such time as may be most agreeable to himself—that he be informed, that, on a view of his conduct throughout the past campaign, and particularly during the period, in which he had the chief command in Virginia, the many new proofs which present themselves of his zealous attachment to the cause he has espoused, and of his judgment, vigilance, gallantry and address in its defence, have greatly added to the high opinion entertained by Congress of his merits and military talents— that he make known to the officers and troops whom he commanded during that period, that the brave and enterprizing services, with which they seconded his zeal and efforts, and which enabled him to defeat the attempts of an enemy, far superior in numbers, have been beheld by Congress, with particular satisfaction and approbation. — That the Secretary of foreign affairs acquaint the Ministers Plenipotentiaries of the United States, that it is the desire of Congress, that they confer with the Marquis Lafayette, and avail of his information, relative to the situation of public affairs in the United States—That the Secretary for foreign affairs, further acquaint the Minister Plenipotentiary at the Court of Versailles, that he will conform to the intention of Congress, by consulting with, and employing the assistance of the Marquis Lafayette, in accelerating the supplies which may be afforded by his most Christian Majesty for the United Stakes—That the superintendent of finance, the Secretary for foreign affairs and the board of war, make such communications to the Marquis, touching the affairs of their respective departments, as will best enable him to fulfill the purpose of the preceding resolutions—That the superintendent of finance, take order for discharging the engagements entered into by the Marquis Lafayette, with the merchants of Baltimore, when he borrowed money of them on his own credit, to supply our troops with necessaries."

At the same time, Congress ordered that a conveyance be provided for General Lafayette, in a public vessel, whenever he should choose to embark; and voted to send a letter by him, to the King of France.

The following is the reply of the Marquis, to the president of Congress, who forwarded him the resolves.

"SIR,

"I have been honored with the resolutions which Congress have been pleased to pass in my favor. Testimonies of their esteem and their confidence that are so very flattering to me, could not but excite those exalted sentiments of gratitude, which I am unable sufficiently to express.—My attachment to America, the sense of my obligations, and the new favors conferred upon me, are so many everlasting ties that devote me to her. At all times, and in every part of the world, my heart will be panting for opportunities to be employed in her service. With unspeakable pleasure, I shall transmit the resolve of Congress to the brave and virtuous troops, whom it has been my happiness to command.

"I have the honor to be, &c.

"LAFAYETTE."

When he transmitted the foregoing resolve of Congress, to the troops he had lately commanded, he observed to them, "In the moment the Major General leaves this place, he wishes once more to express his gratitude to the brave corps of light infantry, who, for nine months past, have been the companions of his fortunes. He can never forget, that, with them alone, of regular troops, he had the good fortune to maneuver before an army, which, after all its reductions, was still six times more numerous than the regular force he had under command."

The interest taken in favour of our country by General Lafayette, and the anxiety he felt upon all occasions for the success of our contest with England, are so strongly evinced by his letter to the Hon. Samuel Adams, that we feel bound in justice to the character of this zealous apostle of liberty, to present it to our readers, with the reply of Mr. Adams. It shows, indeed, not only the disposition of Lafayette, in every possible way, to rapport the cause of America; but his great knowledge of human nature, and his regard for the honorable feelings of soldiers.

The letter was written at Morristown, May 30, 1780, soon after the Marquis returned from his visit to France, where he exerted himself with the French Ministers to grant aid and supplies to the United States.

"*Dear Sir*,—Had I known that I would have the pleasure of meeting you at Boston, and holding confidential conversations with you on public and private matters, I should have anticipated the uneasiness I was put under by the obligation of secrecy, or previously obtained the leave of breaking that so strict law in your favor. Now, my dear sir, that Congress have set my tongue at liberty, at least for such men as Mr. Samuel Adams, I will, in referring you to a public letter from the committee of Congress, indulge my private feelings in imparting to you some confidential ideas of mine on our present situation.

"As momentary visits did not entirely fulfill the purpose of freeing America, France thought they would render themselves more useful, if a naval and land force were sent for co-operating with our troops, and by a longer stay on the coast of the Continent, would give to the states, a fair opportunity of employing all their resources. The expectations are very sanguine at Versailles, and ought to be more so, when that letter shall be received, by which you know *Congress engaged to furnish on their part, five and twenty thousand Continental troops, that are to take the field by the beginning of the spring.*

"On the other hand, my dear sir, all Europe have their eyes upon us: They know nothing of us, but by our own reports, and our first exertions which have heightened their esteem, and by the accounts of the enemy, or those of some dissatisfied persons, which were calculated to give them a quite different opinion: so that, to fix their own minds, all the nations are now looking at us; and the consequence of America, in the eyes of the world, as well as its liberty and happiness, must depend upon the ensuing campaign.

"The succour sent by France, I thought to be *very important* when at Versailles: now that I am on the spot, I know it was *necessary*; and if proper measures are taken, I shall more heartily than ever, enjoy the happiness I had of being somewhat concerned in the operation. But if things stood as they now do, I confess that whether as an American soldier, whether as a private man that said a great deal, and knows Congress have ordered much more to be said on the future exertions of America,—who took a particular delight in praising the patriotic spirit of the United States, I would feel most unhappy and distressed, were I to tell the people that are coming over full of ardour and sanguine hopes, that we have no army to co-operate with them, no provisions to feed the few soldiers that are left, &c. But I hope, my dear sir, it will not be the case; and more particularly depending upon the exertions of your state, *I know Mr. Samuel Adams' influence* and popularity will be as heretofore employed, in the salvation and glory of America.

"If proper measures are taken for provisions, if the states do *immediately* fill up the continental battalions by good drafts, which is by far the best way; if all the propositions of the committee are speedily complied with, I have no doubt, but that the present campaign will be a glorious, decisive one, and that we may hope for every thing that is good: if on the contrary, time be lost, consider what unhappy and dishonorable consequences would ensue from our inability to a co-operation.

"Your state began the noble contest, it may be gloriously ended by your state's exertions, and the example they will once more set to the whole continent. The reception I met with at Boston, binds me to it by the strongest ties of a grateful affection. The joy of my heart will be to find myself concerned in an expedition that may afford peculiar advantages to them; and I earnestly hope it will be the case, in the course of this (if proper measures are taken) glorious campaign.

"I flatter myself you will be yet in Boston, and upon this expectation, I very much depend for the success of the combined expeditions. Such a crisis is worth your being wholly engaged in it, as it will be glorious, important; and I may say it now, because necessary for the support of the great cause in which you acted so early and decisive a part. What you mentioned confidentially to me at Boston, I have duly noticed, and shall ever remember with the attention of a friend. For fulfilling the same purpose, I wish we may be under particular obligations to you on this occasion.

"Give me leave, my dear sir, to suggest to you an idea which I have lately thought of: all the continental officers labor under the most shameful want of clothing. When I say shameful, it is not to them, who have no money to buy—no cloth to be bought. You can conceive what may be theirs and our feelings, when they will be with the French general and other officers; and from a general idea of mankind and human honor it is easily seen how much we should exert ourselves to put the officers of the army in a more decent situation.

"I beg, my dear sir, you will present my respects to your family, and believe me most affectionately,

"Yours,

"LAFAYETTE."

"*Boston, June*, 1780:

"My Dear Marquis,

"Yesterday your very obliging letter of the 30th May was brought to me by
Mons. Guinard.

"The succour coming from France will be so seasonable and important, that if America is not wanting to herself, she will have it in her power by the blessing of heaven, to gratify the utmost of her wishes. His most Christian Majesty's expectations from us must needs be great; and gratitude to so generous an ally as well as a due attention to our own safety, interest and honor, lay us under the strongest obligations to be in readiness to co-operate with the greatest advantage. I have long been fully sensible of your most cordial and zealous attachment to our great cause; and to your personal representation to his Majesty, in addition to the benevolence of his royal heart, I will take the liberty to attribute his design to afford us such aid and for so long a time as may put it in our power to employ all our resources against the enemy.

"It fortunately happened that the General Assembly of this state was sitting when the letter and inclosures from the committee of Congress came to the President of the Council.—They were immediately laid before the Assembly and I have the pleasure to assure you that the filling our battalions by an immediate draft, furnishing the army with provisions, and every other measure for the fulfilling of the just expectations of your sovereign and of Congress, on this most important occasion, are the objects of their closest attention. I had for several months past been flattering myself with the prospect of aid. It strongly impressed my mind from one circumstance which took place when you was at Philadelphia the last year. But far from certainty, I could only express to some confidential friends here, a distant hope, though as I conceived, not without some good effect: at least it seemed to enliven our spirits and animate us for so great a crisis.

"If it were possible for one to be forgetful of our all important cause for a moment, my particular friendship *for you* would be a prevailing inducement with me, to make my utmost feeble exertions to prevent your disappointment after the great pains you have taken to serve us. I have endeavored, and shall continue those endeavors while I stay here, to brighten the dark side of the picture which your imagination has painted in one part of your letter before me—God forbid that we should be obliged to tell our friends when they arrive, that we have not a sufficient army to co-operate with them, nor provisions to feed the few soldiers that are left. I think I may venture to predict that this state will comply with the requisition upon her to give the utmost respectability to our army on so promising an occasion. I was in the Council Chamber when I received your letter, and took the liberty to read some parts of it to the members present. I will communicate other parts of it to some leading members of the House of Representatives as prudence may dictate, particularly what you mention of the officers' want of clothing.

"I thank you my dear sir for the friendly remembrance you had of the hint I gave you when you was here. Be pleased to pay my most respectful compliments to the Commander in Chief, his family, &c. and be assured of the warm affection of your obliged friend and very humble servant,

"SAMUEL ADAMS."

Marquis De Lafayette.

The Legislature of Massachusetts did immediately, viz, on June 5, 1780, pass a resolve for raising four thousand men as a reinforcement of the continental army. The preamble to the resolve was as follows; — "Whereas a requisition has been made to this court for a reinforcement to the continental army, in order that it may be able to act vigorously the ensuing campaign, and the present situation of affairs requiring the utmost exertions at this period, and affords the most flattering prospect of putting an end to this distressing war, if the army is reinforced at this juncture, and enabled to improve the great advantages offered." To carry this resolve into effect, the Brigadier Generals through the State were directed immediately on receipt of the resolve, to issue orders for calling the companies together, and raising the men required from each town, by voluntary enlistments, or by drafting them, on failure of a full number being otherwise raised. Those thus drafted were to be fined if they refused to march; but, a very generous bounty was granted, to induce men to enlist voluntarily. The Selectmen were required to furnish the men with clothes and traveling expenses; and both the Selectmen and Brigadier Generals were liable to a heavy fine, if they neglected their duty. The patriotic efforts of the Legislature, thus drawn into action, in consequence of the pressing letter of Lafayette, and their own sense of the necessity of the case, were every where met by a corresponding zeal on the part of the people of Massachusetts; and the men were soon raised, and sent on to the headquarters of the continental army, to fill the regular regiments of this State, then in the service.

At the siege of York-Town, where Lord Cornwallis with a large British army was attacked and taken by the Americans, Lafayette was particularly distinguished for activity and courage. And a more minute account of this affair is necessary, in recording the useful and brilliant services of this youthful hero in the cause of America, which her sons wish most gratefully to recollect.—General Washington in person commanded the American army on this occasion, in pursuance of a plan he had adopted, as already mentioned. He proceeded to the camp in the vicinity of York-Town, where Cornwallis was posted, the last of September. He was assisted by Major Generals Lincoln, Steuben, Lafayette. Knox, &c. The French troops, who composed a part of the army engaged in the capture of Cornwallis were under command of Count Rochambeau, who had the character of an intelligent and brave officer. The whole number of troops, both American and French, was estimated at twelve thousand. To them, however, were occasionally added small detachments of the militia from the vicinity. The British troops were computed to be about seven thousand, and their commander had been strengthened in his situation by fortifications, hoping to defend himself till he might receive succors from New-York. The allied army was supported in this expedition by a large French fleet which was in the Chesapeake. This afforded great confidence to the Americans, for they had just then defeated the British fleet in those waters, and thus effectually cut off all communication between Lord Cornwallis and the British army in New-York.

The French admiral had been determined to proceed at this time, to a station in the West Indies, agreeably to orders which he had received from the King his master, some weeks before. He was requested to remain, and co-operate in this expedition, by Count Rochambeau, and by Washington himself; but they could not prevail with him to relinquish his proposed departure for the West Indies; and it was only through the most zealous and repeated solicitations of Lafayette, with a solemn promise that he would justify the measure to the Court of France, that the admiral, Count de Grasse, was induced to continue on the station, by which the capture of the British army was greatly facilitated.

Under all these favourable circumstances, it is not unreasonable to suppose, that the allied army cherished a strong confidence of success in their enterprize. Washington had planned this expedition with great intelligence and foresight; for he had been resolved to attempt some decisive and effectual blow against the enemy. He had, however, to engage a body of well disciplined and regular troops under an officer of great experience and bravery; and all his own resources, together with the courage and activity of the officers under his command were necessary to ensure success. The American chief lost no time in preparing for a vigorous attack upon the British. They were soon obliged to abandon their redoubts and advanced posts, and to retire within the town. The light infantry, under General Lafayette, and a party of the French troops, were ordered to advance, and to take possession of the places they had abandoned, that they might cover those of the besieging army who were engaged in throwing up breast works. These advanced parties were much annoyed by a heavy cannonade from the besieged; and Colonel Scammel, the officer of the day, while viewing the ground recently left by the British, was surprised by a party of their cavalry; and, after he surrendered, received a mortal wound, which terminated his life in a few days. Scammel was a brave and accomplished officer, and eminent as a disciplinarian. He was a native of Massachusetts, a gentleman of public education, of elegant manners, and most honorable character. He was greatly lamented by Washington, and by all the officers of the American army. — Those who had been particularly associated with him, long cherished the highest respect for his memory.

Redoubts were thrown up by our advanced parties, for several successive nights; and on the evening of the 7th of October, a large detachment under General Lincoln were ordered out, to open entrenchments near the lines of the British. Lafayette had an important command also in the enterprise. The great interest felt for him by the Americans was shown by a request of the Surgeon General, "that if the Marquis should be wounded, he might receive immediate attention."

The duties of our troops, at this time, were very arduous; but they were most vigilant and active; and by the 9th several batteries were prepared to open upon the town, in which the British General was besieged. General Washington himself put the match to the first gun, and a furious cannonade immediately followed, which was a serious salutation to Cornwallis.

From the 10th to the 15th the siege was prosecuted with great vigor; an incessant fire was kept up by the allied armies; and the enemy were not backward in returning it. The Americans made further approaches to the town and threw up other batteries in a second parallel. Many of our men were killed and wounded in these operations. The enemy had two redoubts, several hundred yards in front of their principal works, which greatly impeded the approaches of the Americans. It became important to obtain possession of them by assault. The one on the left of the enemy's garrison was given to General Lafayette, with a brigade of light infantry of American troops. The other redoubt was attacked by a detachment of French troops under commanded of Baron de Viominel. The assailants, both on the right and left, exhibited the greatest ardor and bravery. Powerful resistance was made by the enemy; but was soon overcome by our gallant troops, inspirited by their still more gallant officers; though with the loss of many of our men. Two field officers were wounded in this affair; one of whom was Major Gibbs from Massachusetts, who then belonged to the guard of the commander in chief. The advanced corps of the detachment on the left, under General Lafayette, was led on to the assault by the intrepid Colonel Hamilton, who during this campaign had command of a regiment of light infantry. Our troops entered the redoubt with charged bayonets, but without firing a gun. The Marquis was indefatigable in pushing forward his men, and was constantly in situations of great peril. Some of the American soldiers were ready to take the lives of the captured after they had possession of the fort, in revenge for the barbarous conduct of the British towards many of our men, and especially for the mortal wound inflicted upon the brave and amiable Scammel, after he had surrendered. General Washington with Lincoln, Knox, and their aids were in the vicinity of this action, in very exposed situations. The Americans under Lafayette, carried the redoubt which they attacked, before the French made their assault upon the other. The latter also, suffered a greater loss of men than the former. When the fort was taken by the troops under the Marquis, he sent his aid, through the fire of the whole British line, to give notice to Baron Viominel, "that he was in his redoubt, and to enquire where the Baron was." The Baron returned for answer, "that he was not yet in his, but should be in five minutes."

General Washington expressed his sense of this brilliant affair in his orders of the 15th, Head Quarters, before York-Town. "The Marquis Lafayette's division will mount the trenches tomorrow. The commander in chief congratulates the allied army on the success of the enterprise, last evening, against the two important redoubts on the left of the enemy's works. He requests the Baron Viominel who commanded the French grenadiers, and the Marquis Lafayette, who commanded the American Light Infantry, to accept his warmest acknowledgments for the excellence of their dispositions, and for their own gallant conduct on the occasion. And he begs them to present his thanks to every individual officer and to the men of their respective commands, for the spirit and rapidity with which they advanced to the points of attack assigned them, and for the admirable firmness with which they supported them, under the fire of the enemy, without returning a shot. The General reflects with the highest pleasure on the confidence which the troops of the two nations must hereafter have in each other: assured of mutual support, he is convinced there is no danger which they will not cheerfully encounter; no difficulty which they will not bravely overcome."

If the Marquis de Lafayette was animated by an ardent love of civil liberty, when he first came to America, his attachment to its principles must have become more firm and settled, if not more intense, after an acquaintance of five years, with the patriots and heroes of our revolution. He had become acquainted with our institutions, and with the principles of our government; and was probably led to believe that systems equally free might be maintained in other countries. He was so enamoured, not only with the theory, but with the practical effects, of republicanism, that he felt it a duty to recommend systems of government more consonant to the rights of mankind. We know not, if he justly appreciated the importance of the general diffusion of knowledge among all classes of people, to ensure such a happy state of society. It was probably owing to this consideration, however, that he did not immediately attempt the reformation of the political system under which his own nation had long been oppressed. That Louis XVI. was mild, humane, and anxious for the good of his subjects, we are not disposed to doubt. But the ancient regime was unquestionably despotic; and in the hands of ambitious or selfish ministers, liable to be an instrument of injustice and oppression. And those who have long been accustomed to govern, without being accountable for their conduct, will not easily be induced to relinquish power, from any considerations of abstract right, or a belief that others will be more just.

We will here present a letter of Lafayette, directed to Sir H. Clinton; to show his regard to truth, and to his own reputation suffering in some measure by a statement which had been publicly made by that military officer.

"Paris, April 29, 1783.—Sir, Upon a perusal of your printed correspondence, I must beg leave to trouble you with an observation; not that I have claims to set forth, or relations to criticise. A sentence in your letter of — — is the only one I intend to mention. "Having said to Lord Cornwallis, that he may be opposed by about 2000 continentals; and, as Lafayette observes, a body of ill-armed militia," you are pleased to add, "as spiritless as the militia of the southern provinces, and without any service;" which reads as if it was a part of my letter. How far your description is undeserving, I think experience has proved; and that it came from me, no American will believe. But your correspondence is so public that with full reliance on your candour and politeness I have taken the liberty to transcribe the passage, and to return it to you, Sir, as its true author. At the same time permit me to assure you, &c.

"LAFAYETTE."

The reply of Sir H. Clinton.

"*London, May* 29, 1783.

"Sir, In consequence of the letter you have done me the honor to write me, I have read over the publication in question; and I confess the remark alluded to, from the manner in which it is introduced, appears to make a part of your letter. You have, certainly, Sir, a right to this acknowledgment, and permit me, at the same time, to add the assurances, &c.

"H. CLINTON."

In the summer of 1784, the Marquis de Lafayette once more visited America. He came to witness the prosperity and improvements of the country; and to enjoy the society of those brave and honorable men, with whom he had been associated in fighting the battles of liberty. Associates in danger form an attachment for each other, which time does not usually destroy. And when they have long struggled together for just and generous purposes, the attachment must be strong and permanent indeed. The heroic actors in our glorious revolution were linked together by the most disinterested ties. They will never forget each other's services and virtues: And we trust, their children will never cease to venerate their characters, or to acknowledge their exalted merit.

When General Lafayette visited the United States in 1784, he was received with an affectionate welcome, little less enthusiastic and splendid, than that with which he has been lately greeted on landing again on our shores, after a lapse of forty years. He then also arrived at the port of New-York; and in October following made a visit to Boston, where he had so many particular friends ready to receive him with the most cordial greetings. He was met at Watertown by the officers of the (then) late continental army, and addressed by his ardent friend, General Knox, in behalf of the whole body, and a public dinner was provided for him on the occasion. The feelings excited by the visit of their beloved fellow officer, will be best described by giving the address; which was as follows:

"We, the late officers of the Massachusetts line of the continental army, embrace the first moment of your arrival, to welcome you with all the sincerity and ardour of fraternal affection: an affection commenced in the dark hour of our conflict, elevated and perfected through the successive vicissitudes of the war.

"We beg leave to observe, that we have had repeated occasions to witness the display of your military talents, and of joining in the approbation and applause which our beloved Commander in Chief so often expressed of your conduct. We are deeply impressed, with a sense of the various and important services you have rendered our country; and it will be the pride of some patriotic and enlightened historian to enumerate your actions in the field, and to illustrate your incessant efforts to promote the happiness of the United States.

"We shall ever retain a lively gratitude for the interposition of your august sovereign and nation, at a time when America was oppressed by a formidable enemy. By his influence and the powerful assistance afforded by his land and naval forces, the war has been happily terminated, and the independence of the United States firmly established, at a period much earlier than the most sanguine patriot could have expected.

"A mind like yours ennobled by a generous attachment to the rights of mankind, must enjoy the highest pleasure in viewing the people, to whose cause you so zealously devoted yourself; in full possession of that peace, liberty and safety, which were the great objects of their pursuit.

"Animated by virtue and the auspices of your own fame, may you go on to add to the splendor of your character, and heighten the glory of your country, by placing the name of Lafayette on the same list with Conde, Turenne and her other immortal heroes.

"In behalf of the officers of the Massachusetts line.

"H. KNOX."

Reply of the Marquis.

"From the instant of our parting, Gentlemen, I have been eagerly looking forward to this period. How far my pleasure is completed by your kind welcome, I leave, my beloved friends, to your own hearts to determine.

"While your affection and confidence ever made me happy, let me gratefully acknowledge, that, for the marks of our beloved General's approbation, I felt myself wholly obliged to the gallant troops I commanded. Could my conduct, in any degree justify your partiality, it will be the pride of my heart to think the American camp was my school, every one of you my brothers, and that I was adopted as a disciple and son, by our immortal Commander in Chief.

"In the interposition of my Sovereign and nation, I enjoyed more than I could express; every French citizen felt with a patriotic King in this happy alliance; and from those troops who shared in our dangers, you meet with a peculiar regard and attachment.

"During my absence, gentlemen, my heart has been constantly with you. As an army, we are separated. But forever, I hope, shall unite in a brotherly affection: and now that a glorious peace has terminated your labours, I rejoice to find your attachment to those principles for which you have conquered, ranks you among the most virtuous citizens of the Commonwealth.

"LAFAYETTE."

At the public dinner given by the officers of the late army to this distinguished friend of American Independence, were also invited the Governor and Council, and many others of high rank and distinction. It may be gratifying to some who peruse this volume to know the sentiments offered as toasts on the joyful occasion. The following are selected:

The United States—His most Christian Majesty.

General Washington—The Cincinnati.

The asserters and supporters of the rights of mankind through the world.

May America never forget in prosperity those what were her fast friends in adversity.

May our country be as famed for justice and honor as she is for valour and success.

The Legislature of the State being in session, ordered, that the Marquis de Lafayette be invited by the President of the Senate and the Speaker of the House of Representatives together with the Supreme Executive to meet the two Houses of Assembly in the Senate room "to congratulate him on his safe arrival in the United States, after the final establishment of peace, to which his friendly influence in Europe had largely contributed." The Marquis attended accordingly, when the Governor congratulated him in terms of the highest respect and affection; to which the Marquis made a polite and suitable reply. But Lafayette was too much beloved and his eminent services in our cause too highly appreciated by the people of the patriotic town of Boston, not to meet with a more general welcome. A dinner was given him at Faneuil-Hall by the citizens; at which were present the Governor and Council, President of the Senate and Speaker of the House of Representatives, the Clergy and other distinguished gentlemen, and seventy five officers of the late continental army. When General Washington's name was given for a toast, the Marquis rose from his seat, and with a tear starting in his eye, began the act of applause, which was continued and repeated again and again by the whole company.

In other places, the Marquis also met a cordial and distinguished reception. His ardent attachment to America and his great services in her cause, were still fresh in the recollection of all. It was known, that be had advocated our independence in Europe, and exerted his influence with his generous Prince to aid in its support. It was remembered, "that in the moment of our greatest misfortunes, he espoused the cause of America," that his military talents and the ardour of his virtuous mind had been devoted to our interest: and "while gratitude should be accounted a virtue, the name of Lafayette," it was said, "would not cease to be dear to Americans."

When about to leave the United States and return to France, Dec. 1784, the Marquis de Lafayette addressed a note to Congress, and expressed a desire to take a respectful leave of that body, before his final departure. A committee was appointed on this request of the Marquis, of which the Hon. Mr. Jay was chairman, and whose report was as follows—"That the merit and services of General Lafayette render it proper that such opportunity of taking leave of Congress be afforded, as may strongly manifest their esteem and regard for him."—Whereupon it was resolved, "That a Committee to consist of a member from each states be appointed to receive the Marquis, and in the name of Congress to take leave of him—that they be instructed to assure him, that Congress continue to entertain the same high sense of his abilities and zeal to promote the welfare of America, both here and in Europe, which they have frequently expressed and manifested on former occasions, and which the recent marks of his attention to their commercial and other interests have perfectly confirmed. That as his uniform and unceasing attachment to this country has resembled that of a patriotic citizen, the United States regard him with particular affection, and will not cease to feel an interest in whatever may concern his honor and prosperity, and that their best and kindest wishes will always attend him."

It was also resolved by Congress, at the same time; "That a letter be written to his most Christian Majesty, and signed by the President of Congress, expressive of the high sense which the United States entertain of the real talents and meritorious services of the Marquis de Lafayette, and recommending him to the particular favor and patronage of his Majesty."

The committee received the Marquis in Congress Hall, and took leave of him in the name of that honorable body, agreeably to the instructions given there. They communicated to him the resolves before mentioned; to which he replied—

"While it pleases the Congress of the United States so kindly to receive me, I want words to express the feelings of a heart, which delights in their present situation and in the public marks of their esteem.

"Since I joined the standard of liberty to this wished for hour of my personal congratulations, I have seen such glorious deeds performed and virtues displayed, by the sons of America, that in the instant of my first concern for them, I had anticipated but a part of the love and regard which devote me to this rising empire.

"During our revolution, I obtained an unlimited, indulgent confidence, which I am equally proud and happy to acknowledge; it dates with the time, when an inexperienced youth, I could only claim my respected friend's paternal adoption. It has been most benevolently continued throughout every circumstance of the cabinet and the field; and in personal friendships I have often found a support against public difficulties. While on this solemn occasion, I mention my obligations to Congress, the States, and the people at large, permit me to remember my dear military companions, to whose services their country is so much indebted.

"Having felt both for the timely aid of my country, and for the part she, with a beloved king, acted in the cause of mankind, I enjoy an alliance so well riveted by mutual affection, by interest and even local situation. Recollection ensures it. Futurity does but enlarge the prospect: and the private intercourse will every day increase, which independent and advantageous trade cherishes, in proportion as it is justly understood.

"In unbounded wishes to America, I am happy to observe the prevailing disposition of the people to strengthen the confederation, preserve public faith, regulate trade; and, in a proper guard over continental magazines and frontier posts, in a general system of militia, in foreseeing attention to the navy, to ensure every kind of safety. May this immense temple of freedom ever stand a lesson to oppressors, an example to the oppressed, a sanctuary for the rights of mankind! And may these happy United States attain that complete splendor and prosperity, which will illustrate the blessings of their government, and for ages to come, rejoice the departed souls of its founders.

"However unwilling to trespass on your time, I must yet present you with my grateful thanks for the late favours of Congress; and never can they oblige me so much, as when they put it in my power, in every part of the world, and to the latest day of my life, to gratify the attachment, which will ever rank me among the most zealous and respectful servants of the United States."

On the return of the Marquis de Lafayette to his native country in 1785, he spent some time in the bosom of his amiable family. With an affectionate wife, of cultivated mind and accomplished manners, with a circle of literary friends, and enjoying a high reputation for his heroic services in America, he must have possessed all the ingredients of human happiness. He received the smiles of the King and Court; was caressed by the gay and chivalrous; and had the esteem and friendship of the first literary characters in France. He was fond of agricultural pursuits; and as his estates were extensive, he devoted a considerable portion of his time to the cultivation and improvement of his lands. During this time his hospitable attentions were shown to American travelers, who were always sure of his friendly reception.

The legislature of Virginia, in 1786, conferred upon Lafayette, an honorable tribute of regard, in recollection of his very important services in defence of American Independence; and particularly of his brave and successful efforts during the campaign of 1781, against Cornwallis. This was a resolution to place his bust in their capitol. Mr. Jefferson, then in France, was authorized to have the like work of honor fixed in Paris, with consent of the municipal authority of that city and accordingly, another bust of Lafayette; was placed, by approbation of the King and of the Provot of Paris, in one of the galleries of the city hall.

In 1786, he traveled through various parts of Germany, and visited the courts of Vienna and Berlin. He became acquainted with Frederick II. the greatest royal tactician of Europe; and probably availed of the opportunity of attending his reviews, to increase his knowledge of military discipline. Soon after his return to France, we find him uniting his influence and efforts with the celebrated philosopher, Malesherbes, who was zealously engaged in favour of the French protestants. At this time, also, he joined a society in Paris, whose object was the gradual emancipation of the unfortunate Africans: so generous and active are the principles of liberty, that they never cease to urge those, who yield to their influence, to deeds of benevolence and humanity. In 1787, he was chosen a deputy to the assembly of the States General, by the nobility of Auvergne, his native province; and at this time he shared largely in the popular favour. But, although subsequently found among the most zealous for a new constitution, by which the power of the monarch was greatly curtailed, he now voted with the other members of the order of nobles, and contended for their distinct authority.

At this meeting of the States General, however, he was active in procuring a favorable decree for the protestants, and was the first to raise his voice for the suppression of *"lettres de cachet."* This convocation of the States General, composed of separate chambers or orders, had not been long in session, when great difficulties arose in consequence of various plans, and the conflicting opinions of different factions, (for factions were now beginning to appear;) and it was proposed to call a "National Assembly." It does not appear, that this was a favorite measure of Lafayette; though, from his avowed sentiments respecting the equal rights of man, it cannot be doubted, that he approved of the plan. For in 1789, he became a member of this celebrated assembly, whose acts not only laid the foundation, for a radical change in the government of France, but tended directly to destroy the whole power of the monarch. Even here, indeed, he appeared as the friend and advocate of Louis; and however ardent he was for an amelioration of the condition of the people, by rendering the civil government more mild, than heretofore, he was sincere and active in providing for the personal safety of his Prince, and for the honor of his crown, conformably to his views of political liberty.

He had, in truth, a most difficult part to act. He was ardently attached to the cause of freedom, and wished the people should have the public enjoyment of their just and national principles. And he was equally desirous, that his royal master should still retain such a portion of authority, as would be requisite to the dignity of the first magistrate of a great nation.—But the accomplishment of such generous sentiments was utterly impossible. Neither Louis, nor his courtiers could consent to the limitations of the royal authority, proposed by the reformers, and which were necessary to a just exercise of power in the people, whose representatives should share in the administration of the government. And many of the leaders in the revolution, even in its incipient stage, on the other hand, had such ambitious views, or visionary projects, that nothing would satisfy them, but an entire relinquishment of power long claimed and exercised by the Kings of this ancient nation.

In 1789, the new constitution was proposed by the National Assembly, by which the distinct and independent power of the monarch was almost annihilated; and the whole legislative authority was given to the representatives of the people. That Lafayette, and some others who advocated this instrument, were actuated by a disinterested love of the people, and believed that sufficient power was reserved to the King to secure respect for him, as the political head of the nation, cannot be doubted. We have only to lament, that subsequent events afforded proofs of the unfitness of the French people, at that period, for the blessings of a more popular government. It must also be admitted, that many who professed republicanism, and boasted of their regard to the people's rights were unprincipled and ambitious men, whom power had intoxicated, or who entertained views of government utterly inconsistent with the just authority of the laws, and the safety of individuals. Lafayette offered the declaration of the rights of man, at this period, for the sanction of the assembly: And though he was accused by the anti-revolutionists, as the author of all the excesses and cruelties which followed, for this proposition, it may justly be said in his behalf, that it contained no other axioms, than are admitted, by all impartial writers, as essential in free governments. The King and his courtiers condemned them; and jacobins and demagogues afterwards abused them, in their wild notions of republicanism, or their selfish projects of personal aggrandizement.

Lafayette was charged with indiscretion and want of judgment, for the active and zealous part which he took in the revolution, not only by bigoted monarchists, but by some who were friendly to republican institutions. He is said to have declared, "that when oppression and tyranny were at their height, insurrection became a duty." This declaration, however, when candidly considered, implies no more, than was frequently expressed by the patriots of America, when opposing the arbitrary power of the British ministry, and advocating independence as the only remedy. The ardour and enthusiasm of Lafayette, probably, betrayed him into some practical errors, and led him to utter expressions, which were capable of being pressed into the service of jacobins and anarchists. We only contend, that he had no selfish views to accomplish—and that he was really friendly to the welfare and honor of his Prince, as well as to the liberty and happiness of the French people.

This is fully established by the fact, that, at this period and afterwards, when jacobin clubs were formed and acted as dictators to the National Assembly, he became obnoxious to them, for his firmness in adhering to constitutional principles; and, though generally censured by the royalists as an advocate for liberty and reform, was hated and opposed by the factions, with the pretence of his being still attached to the ancient regime. He retained his hold on the affections of the people for some time, and enjoyed also, more of the confidence and regard of the King, then any other who had favored the revolution. The court found him, at least, candid and sincere; and he often exposed himself to imminent danger in their defence. As proof of the former, he was chosen Vice President of the national assembly, in the absence of the aged President, July 1789; and appointed to the command of the citizens of Paris, to quell the riots, and to restore tranquility to the city, when an alarming tumult existed, in consequence of the want of bread among the lower classes. As evidence of the latter, the King often consulted him in cases of difficulties and danger; and entrusted his person and family to his custody, when threatened by a lawless mob, though he well knew the sentiments of Lafayette, on the great question of royal authority.

When he was appointed to the command of the Parisian militia, (afterwards denominated the national guard,) which had been promptly organized according to a plan of his suggesting, it was a time of great confusion and tumult. He accepted the appointment from the most patriotic motives. Drawing his sword before an immense concourse of citizens then assembled, "Lafayette made a vow to sacrifice his life, if necessary, to the preservation of that precious liberty which had been entrusted to him." It was then too, at the moment of his "brightest popularity," that he exhorted those who pressed around him, "to love the friends of the people; but, at the same time, to maintain an entire submission to the laws, and to cherish a zeal for liberty."

He manifested the highest respect for the civil power, even when he commanded the national guard and Parisian militia, though with this immense military force, and with his unbounded popularity, he might have safely followed his own wishes. The Parisians were eager to march to Versailles, where the King and court resided, to demand an immediate supply of bread. The mob proceeded thither in great numbers, and still greater tumult. He declined marching the military, until be had the express consent and order of the National Assembly. And on his arrival, he immediately joined with the king's body guard, in suppressing the riotous proceedings of the promiscuous multitude, who had previously reached the place, and were committing depredations even in the royal palace. This was a scene of great confusion and alarm; and violence and bloodshed ensued. The enemies of Lafayette pretended, that he might have prevented the mischief, by timely and decisive measures. But impartial witnesses testified, "that, from the first moment of the alarm, he had even exceeded his usual activity." He appeared in every quarter. "Gentlemen," said he to the Parisian soldiers, "I have pledged my word and honor to the King, that nothing belonging to him shall receive injury. If I break my word, I shall no longer be worthy of being your commander." The people insisted, that the King should go to Paris; and on consulting with the Marquis, who gave assurances of protection and respect, he proceeded to the city, accompanied by his family, and was received with great acclamations of *vive Le Roi.*

Lafayette still retained his great popularity and influence. The Court party had perfect confidence in his integrity and honor, though they did not approve of his revolutionary principles. And the friends of the constitution found in him one of their most zealous and able supporters. These, however, soon become divided into clubs and parties; some of whom were aiming at more power for the representatives of the people, and for divesting Louis of every thing but the name of King. To this description of politicians, Lafayette, and others who constituted the majority of the National Assembly at this time, were opposed. They considered the King as still the fountain of all executive authority, and were willing that he should also have a *veto* upon their legislative proceedings—His person, they declared, was inviolable, and his crown hereditary. Put the more violent revolutionists, who soon became known by the distinctive appellation of *Jacobins*, formed themselves into a club; where extravagant measures were proposed and then presented to the assembly; and frequently were adopted, through intrigue and threats, when a majority of the members were dissatisfied with them.

Attached to the constitution, a friend to justice and order, and an advocate for the dignity and authority of the monarch, as limited and defined by the constitution, Lafayette was among the most open and decided in counteracting the views of the Duc de Orleans, Mirabeau, Petion, Brissot, Robespeirre, and others of the jacobin faction, who aimed at further changes to fulfill their own selfish and ambitious designs. Orleans was an unprincipled and dangerous nobleman; of royal blood and cousin to Louis: But his object was to bring about an entire revolution, and place himself on the throne of France. He, therefore, hated and feared Lafayette; who, he knew, was too honest to further his plans, and too powerful to allow him to succeed: Orleans became obnoxious and was persuaded to leave the kingdom. But he soon returned; and promoted or approved the shocking excesses which were afterwards committed.

During the years 1790 and 1791 great agitations existed in Paris, on various occasions, through the changing opinions of political leaders, and the collisions of individuals, who were rivals for power. The grand confederation took place in July 1790, when the constitution received the sanction of all classes; and when Lafayette, at the head of the national guards, attracted as much notice and possessed as great influence as the king himself. His popularity seemed unbounded; nor did he commit any act of cruelty or injustice to injure his high reputation. He could not, in all instances, command the military or restrain the mob; but he had the merit of using his greatest efforts to preserve order, and to maintain the authority of the laws. When the King proposed to visit St. Cloud, he was opposed by the populace and the Jacobin clubs, under the pretence that he intended to leave the kingdom. Lafayette attempted to disperse them and to remove all obstructions to the intended visit of Louis. The troops were disobedient to his orders, and refused to favor the King's journey. Mortified by their insubordination, Lafayette resigned his command, but afterwards resumed it, through the solicitations of the National Assembly, and of the guards themselves, who regretted their disobedience of his orders.

On the attempt of the King, soon after, to depart from France, who had become disgusted with the conduct of the revolutionists, and was in fear of his personal safety, Lafayette was charged with being privy to the plan, and subjected himself to the popular displeasure on this suspicion. That he promoted the plan, was never proved, and is not probable. That he had intimations of it, is possible; but that he gave strict orders to the officers about the king's palace to guard against such an event is most certain. He discharged his duty as a public agent; and it is not improbable he might have supposed the king in immediate danger, and that by a temporary absence from the capital, the ferment would subside, and he might return in safety. No one, for a moment, believed that he wished, with the emigrants and other enemies of the revolution, to have Louis surrender himself to the hostile powers of the coalition, for the purpose of bringing a foreign army to enslave France. He was, indeed, anxious for the safety of his Prince; but he would never have compromitted the liberties of his country, even for such an object.

From this period, the Jacobin clubs became more popular, and had the chief direction of all political affairs. In their desire to lesson the authority of the King, and to secure power, they hesitated at no measures, however unjust; and the new constitution, even which they had sworn to support, was grossly violated in the prosecution of their selfish views. The influence of Lafayette was rapidly undermined by these artful demagogues. He was sincerely attached to the constitution; and was desirous of maintaining inviolate; the power of the, monarch which it guaranteed. He was the friend to law, and opposed all his influence to riots and excesses. He became an object of dread to the Jacobins, and they resolved to destroy him. But for a long time, the majority of the National Assembly supported him. In attempting to suppress a dangerous riot, by which many of the citizens were alarmed and threatened, when he commanded the military in 1791, he was shot at by one of the mob. The man was taken, and he forgave him—But the National Assembly decreed the death of the culprit, who had attempted the life of "the hero of the day." And the municipality of Paris, also had a gold medal struck off, in honor of Lafayette, and presented him with a bust of Washington in approbation of his conduct.

He was repeatedly denounced by individuals of the violent party, before they succeeded in rendering him obnoxious to popular displeasure. And this was finally effected, through misrepresentations and false reports.

Letter of Lafayette, Feb. 1791, to M. de Bonille, one of the court, but not then at Paris.

"Paris is divided by factions, and the kingdom oppressed by anarchy. The violent aristocrats dream of a counter revolution—the clergy concur with them. The impartial monarchists are looking for a part to play, without the means of doing it. Among the friends of the revolution, you have many honest men, some lose themselves in speculations—and some Jacobins, whose leaders spread trouble everywhere. As to the ministers, they are merged in the revolution; and have no rule, but to yield to the popular voice. The Queen is resigned to the revolution,—hoping that opinions will soon change. The King wishes the happiness of the people, and the general tranquility, to begin his own. As to myself, I am attacked by all the party leaders, who consider me an obstacle not to be overcome or intimidated. Add to this, the hatred of the aristocrats and of the Orleans party; of the Lameths, with whom I was formerly connected; of Mirabeau, who says I despise him; the money distributed, the libels, the dissatisfaction I give those whom I prevent from pillaging Paris—and you will have the sum of all which is going on against me. But except a few ardent heads who are mislead, the well meaning, from the highest to the lowest, are for me.

"I stand well with the National Assembly, except a few disreputable Jacobins. I have little connexion with the court, for I can derive no use from it to my country; and yet I am aware advantage is taken of my neglect to intrigue. Some friends are at work with me, upon a plan of conduct, by which the revolution will be consolidated, the good basis of the constitution established, and public order restored. The chief talents of the assembly, Mirabeau himself, cannot but support this plan. Here then are courts established, and juries are decreed; this is the moment to let our voice be heard with force, propriety and utility.

"You have accepted the coalition which my heart and my patriotism have offered you. You lately said to one of my friends, "If Lafayette and I understand each other well, we shall establish a constitution."

"My first wish is to finish the revolution speedily and well, to secure the constitution on solid foundations, to employ for that purpose, all I possess of national confidense and personal means; and then to be nothing more in France, than an active citizen. Adieu,

"LAFAYETTE."

But after he was persecuted by the Petions and Robespieres of the day, because of his moderation, loyalty and attachment to the constitution, he was held in high esteem by the friends of rational freedom, and still enjoyed the confidence both of Louis and of the National Assembly. Toward the close of the year 1791, by request of the King, he was appointed to command the army of the centre, to oppose the foreign troops then invading France. When he accepted the appointment, he assured the National Assembly of his "determination to support the constitution." The President replied, "the French nation, who have sworn to conquer and to live free, will always, with confidence, present to their foes and to tyrants, the constitution and Lafayette."

As commander in chief of that department of the French army entreated to him, he was assiduous to maintain proper discipline and order; a matter of great difficulty, as a revolutionary spirit pervaded all ranks, and the soldiers were disposed to insubordination, especially under a leader not belonging to the popular party. He had several engagements with the enemy, in which he was successful. But his operations and those of the other generals, who commanded in other departments of the northern armies of France, were greatly impeded by the injudicious and variable plans of the assembly, then torn by factions, and disgraced by low intrigues. The evil spirit extended to the military; and each faction had its partizans among the soldiers. Lafayette saw and lamented this disastrous state of things; and he dared to oppose his single efforts to avert the impending ruin. It was at this time, that he wrote his celebrated letter to the National Assembly, of June 16, 1792, in which he exposed the violence and the cabals of the Jacobins, and conjured the moderates to cling to the constitution, as the only means of safety. This letter is so important, in developing the views and sentiments of Lafayette, and in detecting the causes of the excesses, which eventually disgraced the French revolution of that period, that it will be proper to record it in this connexion. He wrote to the King at the same time, expressing great anxiety for his safety, and declaring his wish to maintain the constitution.

Lafayette's letter to the Legislative body.

"*At the entrenched camp of Maubeuge*, 16_th June_, 1792.

"GENTLEMEN,

"At the moment, perhaps too long deferred, in which I am about to call your attention to the highest public interests, and to point out among our dangers, the *conduct of a ministry*, whom I have for a long time censured in my correspondence, I learn that, unmasked in consequence of its own divisions, it has fallen a sacrifice to its own intrigues. [This was the Brissotin ministry.] It is not enough however, that *this branch* of the government has been delivered from its disastrous influence. The public welfare is in peril—The fate of France depends principally on its representatives—The nation expects from them its security. But in giving them a *constitution*, France has prescribed to them the *only* means by which she can be saved.

"Persuaded, gentlemen, that as the rights of man are the law of every constituent assembly, a constitution ought to be the law of the legislators, which that constitution shall have established. It is to you that I ought to denounce the too powerful efforts which are making, to induce you to depart from that course which you have promised to pursue.

"*Nothing shall deter me from the exercise of this right of a free man, to fulfill this duty of a citizen*; neither the momentary errors of opinion; for what are opinions when they depart from principles: nor my respect for the *representatives* of the people; for I respect still more the *people*, whose sovereign will it is to have a constitution: nor the benevolence and kindness which you have constantly evinced for myself; for I would *preserve* that as I *obtained* it, by an inflexible love of liberty.

"Your situation is difficult—France is menaced from without, and agitated within. Whilst foreign powers announce the intolerable (inadmissible) project of attacking our national sovereignty, and avow it as a principle! at the same time the enemies of France, its interior enemies, intoxicated with fanaticism and pride, entertain chimerical hopes, and annoy us with their insolent malevolence. You ought, gentlemen, to repress them; and you will have the power so to do, *only when* you shall become *constitutional* and *just.* You wish it, *no doubt*; but cast your eyes upon all that passes within your own body and around you. Can you dissemble even to yourselves, that a *faction*, (and to avoid all vague denunciations) the *jacobin faction*, have caused all these disorders? It *is that which I boldly accuse* — organized like a separate empire in the metropolis, and in its affiliated societies, blindly directed by some ambitious leaders, this sect forms a *corporation entirely distinct* in the midst of the French people, whose powers it usurps, by tyrannizing over its representatives and constituted authorities.

"It is in that body, in its public meaning, the *love* of the laws is denounced as aristocracy, and their *breach* as patriotism. *There* the assassins of Dessilles receive their triumphs, the crimes of Jourdan find panegyrists. There, the recital of the massacre which has stained the city of Metz, has also been received with *infernal* acclamations! Have they become sacred because the emperor Leopold has pronounced their name? And because it is our highest duty to combat the *foreigners*, who mingle in our domestic quarrels, are we at liberty to refrain from *delivering* our country from domestic tyranny?

"Of what importance is it, as to the fulfillment of this duty, that strangers have their projects; and their connivance and concert with our internal foes? It is I, who denounce to you this sect [the jacobins]; I, who, without speaking of my past life, *can reply* to those who suspect my motives—"Approach, in this moment of awful crisis, when the character of each man must be known, and see which of us, more inflexible in his principles, more obstinate in his resistance, will more courageously overcome, those obstacles, and those dangers, which traitors to their country conceal, and which true citizens know how to appreciate, and to brave for her."

"And how could I delay longer to fulfill this duty, whilst every successive day weakens still more the constituted authorities, substitutes the spirit of party for the will of the people; whilst the audacity of the agitators, [the disorganizers] imposes silence on peaceable citizens, throws into retirement useful men, and whilst *devotion* to the *sect* or *party* stands in the place of *public* and *private* virtues, which, in a free country, ought to be the austere [severe, or strict] and only means of attaining to public office.

"It is, after having opposed to all the obstacles, and to all the snares, which were laid for me, the courageous and persevering patriotism of an army, sacrificed perhaps to conspiracies against its commander, (Lafayette was the commander) that I now oppose to this faction the *correspondence* of a *ministry, worthy* representative of its *club*—a correspondence, the calculations of which are false, its promises vain and illusory—its information deceitful or frivolous— its advice perfidious or contradictory—correspondence, in which *after* pressing me to advance without precaution—to attack *without means*—they finally began to tell me that *resistance* was *impossible,* when I indignantly repelled the cowardly and base assertion. What a remarkable conformity of language, gentlemen, between the factions whom the *aristocracy* avow, and those who *usurp* the *name* of *patriots!* They both wish to overthrow our laws, rejoice in our disorders, array themselves against the constituted authorities, detest the national guards (the militia)—preach insubordination to the army— sow, at one moment, distrust, at another, discouragement.

"As to myself, gentlemen, *who embraced the American cause at the moment when its ambassadors declared to me that it was perilous or desperate—* who from that moment have devoted my life to a persevering defence of liberty and of the sovereignty of the people—who, on the 14th of July, 1789 after the taking of the Bastille, in presenting to my country a declaration of rights dared to say "that in order that a nation should be free, it is only necessary that it should *will* so to be." I come, this day, full of confidence in the justice of our cause— of contempt, for the cowards who desert it, and of indignation against the traitors who would sully or stain it with crimes; I am ready to declare that the French nation, if it is not the vilest in the universe, can and ought to resist the conspiracy of kings who have coalesced against it!

"It is not in the midst of my brave army that timid counsels should be permitted.—Patriotism, discipline, patience, mutual confidence, all the military and civil virtues I find here. Here the principles of liberty and equality are cherished, the laws respected, property held sacred. Here calumnies and factions are unknown. And when I reflect that France has many millions who can become *such* soldiers, I ask myself, to what a degree of *debasement* must such an immense people be reduced, stronger in its natural resources than in its artificial defences, opposing to a monstrous and discordant confederation, simple and united counsels and combinations, that the cowardly, degrading idea of sacrificing its soverignty, of permitting any discussion as to its liberties, of committing to negotiation its rights, could be considered among the *possibilities* of a rapidly advancing futurity!

"But, in order that we, soldiers of liberty, should combat for her with efficacy, or *die* for her with any *fruit* or advantage, it is necessary that the number of the defenders of the country should be promptly made in some degree proportionate to that of our opponents; that the supplies of all descriptions should be increased so as to facilitate our movements; that the comfort and conveniences of the troops, their clothes and arms, their pay, the accommodations for the sick, should no longer be subject to fatal delays, or to a miserable and misplaced economy, which defeats its very end.

"It is *above all, necessary* that the citizens rallied round their constitution, should be assured that the rights which that constitution guarantees shall be respected with a *religious* fidelity; which will of itself cause more despair to our enemies than any other measure.

"Do not repel this desire—this ardent wish. It is that of all the sincere friends of your legitimate authority; assured that no *unjust* consequence or effect can flow from a *pure* principle—that no tyrannical measure can save a cause, which owes its *force*, aye, and its glory, to the sacred principles of liberty and equality. Let criminal jurisprudence resume its *constitutional* power. Let civil equality—let religious freedom enjoy the application of their true principles. In fine, let the reign of the *clubs* be *annihilated* by you; let them give place to the laws—*their* usurpations to the firm and independent exercise of the powers of the constituted authorities—their disorganizing maxims to the true principles of liberty—their delirious fury to the calm and constant courage of a nation which knows its rights, and is ready to defend them—in fine, their sectarian combinations to the true interests of the country, of the nation, which in a moment of danger ought to unite *all*, except those, to whom its subjection and ruin are the objects of atrocious pleasure and infamous speculation.

"LAFAYETTE."

"Camp of Maubeuge, June, 16, 1792.

"SIRE—I have the honor to send your Majesty the copy of a letter to the National Assembly, in which you will find expressed the sentiments which have animated me all my life. The King knows with what ardour and perseverance I have at all times been devoted to the cause of liberty and to the principles of humanity, equality and justice. He knows, that I have always been the adversary of *faction*, the enemy of licentiousness, and that no power which I thought illegal has ever been acknowledged by me. He is acquainted with my devotion to his constitutional authority, and with my attachment to his person. Such, Sire, were the grounds of my letter to the National Assembly; such shall be those of my conduct to the nation and your Majesty, amidst the storms raised around to by hostile or by factious combinations.

"It does not belong to me, Sire, to give greater importance to my opinions and actions, than what is due to the individual conduct of a simple citizen. But the expression of my thoughts was always a right, and on this occasion becomes a duty; and though I should have performed it sooner, if, instead of being in a camp, I had remained in that retirement from which I was forced by the dangers of my country: yet I do not think that any public employment or private consideration exempts me from exercising this duty of a citizen, this right of a freeman.

"Persist, Sire, supported by the authority delegated to you by the national will, in the noble resolution of defending constitutional principles against all their enemies. Let this resolution, maintained by all the actions of your private life, as well as by a firm and complete exercise of the royal power; become the pledge of the harmony, which, particularly, at this critical juncture, cannot fail to be established between the *elected* representatives of the people and their *hereditary* representative. It is in this resolution, Sire, that glory and safety will be found for the country and for yourself. With this you will find the friends of liberty, all *good* Frenchmen ranged around your throne, to defend it against the plots of rebels and the enterprizes of the factious; and I, Sire, who in their honorable hatred have found the reward of my persevering opposition; I will always deserve it, by my zeal in the cause to which my whole life has been devoted, and by my fidelity to the oath I have taken to the nation, to the law and to the King. Such, Sire, are the unalterable sentiments I present to your Majesty, with my respect.

"LAFAYETTE"

Letter of Lafayette on leaving Paris to join his army, after having appeared at the bar of the National Assembly, and protested against their proceedings, the last of June.

"Gentlemen—In returning to the post where brave soldiers are ready to die for the constitution, but ought not and will not lavish their blood except for that, I go with great and deep regret in not being able to inform the army, that the National Assembly have yet deigned to come to any determination on my petition. [alluding to the request in his letter to the assembly a short time before, to suppress the Jacobin clubs.] The voice of all the good citizens of the kingdom, which some factious clamours strive to stifle, daily call to the elected representatives of the people, that while there exists near them a sect who fetter all the authorities, and menace their independence; and who, after provoking war, are endeavoring, by changing the nature of our cause, to make it impossible to defend it; that while there is cause to blush at the impunity of an act of treason against the nation, which has raised just and great alarms in the minds of all the French, and universal indignation; our liberty, laws and honor are in danger. Truths like these, free and generous souls are not afraid of speaking. Hostile to the factious of every kind, indignant at cowards that can sink so low as to look for foreign interposition, and impressed with the principle, which I glory in being the first to declare to France, *that all illegal power is oppression, against which resistance becomes a duty*, we are anxious to make known our fears to the legislative body. We hope that the prudence of the representatives of the people will relieve our minds of them. As for me, gentlemen, who will never alter my principles, sentiments or language, I thought that the National Assembly, considering the urgency and danger of circumstances, would permit me to add my regrets and wishes to my profound respect."

Noble and generous sentiments, worthy of the disciple of our great Washington—'worthy of the philanthropic hero and firm friend of civil liberty'—worthy of the adopted citizen of free and independent America! Such were the opinions and sentiments of Washington and his friends, in 1794, when our republic was assailed by foreign emissaries, and convulsed by secret associations at home, who through ignorance or design were advocates for measures which would have thrown our country into a state of anarchy and misrule.

There was still a small majority in the National Assembly who were the friends of constitutional liberty, and advocates of Lafayette. But the Jacobins were every day increasing; and they felt confident of the popular favor. Enraged at his bold and independent conduct, and suspecting, perhaps that he was a secret supporter of all the wishes of the King, they denounced Lafayette as a traitor and an enemy to the republic. In this state of extreme ferment, while he was openly threatened and every attempt was making to render him odious to the populace, he had the courage (some might say, the rashness) to proceed to Paris, and present himself to the bar of the National Assembly. Few men, in such a situation, would have thus hazarded their lives; but he was strong in conscious rectitude. He appeared before his enemies with dignity and firmness. "He entreated the assembly to come forward and save the country from ruin, by dissolving the factious clubs and inflicting exemplary punishment on the authors of the late disgraceful riots." His friends were numerous in the Assembly, and probably the greater number condemned the violent transactions, against which he raised his voice in the legislative hall of the nation. The national guards in Paris, also, manifested their attachment to Lafayette. They assembled before the hotel in which he lodged; and planting a tree of liberty before the door, which they decorated with ensigns and ribbons, they greeted him with enthusiastic applause. But he was destined to suffer a reverse of fortune, and to be the subject of the most unjust and cruel persecution. The violent party prevailed: Lafayette and constitutional liberty, were proscribed; and the spirit of anarchy and misrule dictated the violent proceedings which deluged France in blood.

Lafayette, finding all his attempts to restore order and to maintain the constitution in vain, speedily returned to the army on the frontiers. This must have been a moment of great anxiety and suspense. Some suppose that, attached as most of the military were to him and supported by his friends of the moderate party, if he had marched his troops to Paris he might have defended the King from indignity, and restored the reign of law. But this is doubtful. The probability is, that with his love of justice and his correct principles, he could not persuade himself "that the end would justify the means;" and that he chose rather to submit to a cruel destiny, than to violate the constitution he had sworn to support, by resorting to physical force for the accomplishment of honorable purposes, and to be the occasion even indirectly of increasing the misery, in which his unhappy country was involved. He was, indeed, accused by his enemies of a design to march to Paris with his troops and to force the assembly into a compliance with his views. But this was a most unfounded calumny. When the minister for the home department wrote to him on the subject, in the name of the Assembly he replied — "If I were questioned respecting my principles, I should say, that as a constant proclaimer and defender of the rights of man, and the sovereignty of the people, I have every where and always resisted authorities which liberty disavowed and which the national will had not delegated; and that I have every where and always obeyed those, of which a free constitution had fixed the forms and the limits. But I am questioned respecting a fact — Did I propose to Marshal Luckner to march to Paris with our armies? To which I answer in four words — *It is not true.*"

Under the pretence that General Lafayette was meditating some plan hostile to the cause of liberty, or designed to aid the King in another attempt to escape from France, three commissioners were sent to counteract his movements. But he was notified of their appointment, and ordered their arrest before they reached his army.

He knew they were deputed by a faction, and hoped the assembly would return to more moderate and just views. He addressed the following letter to the troops under his command. "It is no longer time to conceal from you what is going forward. The constitution you swore to maintain is no more; a troop of factious men besieged the palace of the Tuilleries; the national and Swiss guards made a brave resistance, but they were obliged to surrender, and were inhumanly murdered. The King, Queen and all the royal family escaped to the National Assembly; the factious ran thither, holding a sword in one hand and fire in the other, and forced the legislative body to supersede the King, which was done for the sake of saving his life. Citizens, you are no longer represented; the National Assembly are in a state of slavery; Petion reigns; the savage Danton and his satellites are masters. Thus it is for you to determine whether you will support the hereditary representative of the throne, or submit to the disgrace of having a Petion for your king."

The appeal was in vain. Though a momentary respond was given by the soldiers to the sentiments of their magnanimous commander, the baleful influence of faction had corrupted many of them; and finding himself robbed of the confidence of the army, as well as of the assembly, and thus deprived of all hope of being useful to his country, he quitted France, with an intention of retiring to America, where he had just reason to expect a grateful reception.

Thus terminated the revolutionary career of Lafayette; through the whole of which he appears to the impartial observer to have acted an honorable and disinterested part. If he committed faults, they were those of opinion or judgment; in sincerity and in zealous devotion to the liberty of his country, he was exceeded by none. He may justly be considered "an illustrious confessor of regulated liberty." His great object was to reform existing abuses, to lay the foundation of constitutional freedom: and with all his zeal for the recognition and the support of the rights of man, he was desirous of preserving a just measure of authority in the crowns and maintaining a sacred regard to law and justice. That he failed in his wishes of introducing into France a more mild and popular government, is matter of regret with the friends of civil liberty in America. But he cannot justly be censured by them for the failure of his object, or for the excesses which attended the revolution. The violent proceedings of the jacobins, which excited so much horror among the friends of regulated liberty in other countries, were opposed by him personally with singular firmness and constancy. He distinguished, with great accuracy, between the will of the people and the clamours of a faction; and between the deliberate acts of the legislature sanctioned by the constitution, and the hasty sentence or orders of a party, adopted without the usual forms of law, so necessary to the order and welfare of society.

Lafayette was arrested by an Austrian General, and delivered over to the King of Prussia, who ordered him to be confined in a prison at Wesel and at Magdeburg. Here he suffered some time, when he was removed to the fortress of Olmutz. In this place he was kept under the most rigorous confinement— enduring the privations and severity fit only to be inflicted on the greatest criminals.

After a close confinement of several weeks in the common prison at Wesel, he was removed to Magdeburg, and thence to Olmutz. At Magdeburg he was confined for a year, in a dark and solitary dungeon; during which he was offered his liberty, on condition of his joining with the enemies of France. He spurned the proposal with indignation; and preferred imprisonment and indignity, to treachery or hostility to his own country. When first taken into custody, he was treated with insult by the people of some places through which he was conducted; but afterwards, a deep interest was manifested in his behalf, and the warmest sympathy was expressed for his unfortunate condition.

The following is an extract from a letter of Lafayette in 1793, while confined at Magdeburg.

"Since my captivity, but one political paper has reached me, and that is yours for February. I appreciate, with deep sensibility, the justice you render my sentiments, and the approbation you bestow upon my conduct. Your commendations are greatly beyond my deserts; but your kind exaggerations contain, at this moment, something so generous, I cannot withhold from you my thanks, that you have enabled me to hear the voice of liberty honoring my tomb. My situation is peculiarly strange. I have sacrificed my republican partialities to the state and wishes of the nation: I obeyed the sovereign power where I found it vested, in the constitution. My popularity was as great as I could desire; for the legislative body defended me better on the 8th of August, than it defended itself on the 10th. But I became obnoxious to the *Jacobins*, because I reprobated their aristocracy, which aimed at usurping all legitimate authority.

"From Constantinople to Lisbon, from Kamschatka to Amsterdam, every bastille is ready to receive me. The Huron and Iroquois forests are peopled with my friends; the despots and the courts of Europe, they are the only savages I fear. I am aware that the laws of England would protect me, though the court of St. James is opposed to me: but I cannot seek protection in a country at war with my own. *America*, the country of my heart, would welcome me with joy. Yet my fears for the future destiny of France, induce me to give the preference to Switzerland, at least for the present."

After this, he was confined about four years in the prison of Olmutz, when Henry Bollman, a young German physician, and Francis Huger, an American, (son of Colonel Huger, of South Carolina, who had first received Lafayette when he arrived in the United States, in 1777,) made great personal sacrifices, and exposed themselves to imminent dangers to effect his escape. General Washington also, then President of the United States, repeatedly solicited his release, on the ground of his being an American citizen, as he really was by a legal adoption. But his requests were vain. It was not consistent with the policy of the "Legitimates" of Europe, to show any favor to such a friend of liberty as Lafayette, or to listen to the honorable application of the chief magistrate of the American republic.

We have already seen frequent proofs of the peculiar regard which Washington cherished for Lafayette. He did not forget him when immured in the prison at Olmutz. Such was the state of political affairs in Europe, such the suspicions both of the jacobins in France, and the advocates for monarchy in the surrounding nations, that a formal and public request for the release of Lafayette, would have been of no avail. It would probably have added to the severity of his treatment by his implacable enemies. The American ministers residing at foreign courts were instructed, however, to suggest on proper occasions, the wishes of the President of the United States, for his enlargement. A confidential person was sent to Berlin to solicit his discharge. But Lafayette had been placed in the custody of the Austrian cabinet, before the messenger arrived. The American envoy at the court of St. James, exerted himself in favour of the heroic friend of Washington, but without effect. As the last resource, the President wrote directly to the Emperor of Germany on the subject. Justice both to Washington and Lafayette requires the recital of the letter.

"It will readily occur to your majesty, that occasions may sometimes exist, on which official considerations would constrain the chief of a nation to be silent and passive in relation even to objects which affect his sensibility, and claim his interposition as a man. Finding myself precisely in this situation at present, I take the liberty of writing this private letter to your majesty, being persuaded that my motives will also be my apology for it.

"In common with the people of this country, I retain a strong and cordial sense of the services rendered to them by the Marquis de Lafayette; and my friendship for him has been constant and sincere. It is natural, therefore, that I should sympathize with him and his family in their misfortunes; and endeavour to mitigate the calamities they experience, among which his present confinement is not the least distressing.

"I forbear to enlarge on this delicate subject. Permit me only to submit to your majesty's consideration, whether his long imprisonment and the confiscation of his estate, and the indigence and dispersion of his family, and the painful anxieties incident to all these circumstances, do not form an assemblage of sufferings which recommend him to the mediation of humanity? Allow me, Sir, on this occasion to be its organ; and to entreat that he may be permitted to come to this country, on such conditions as your majesty may think it expedient to prescribe.

"As it is a maxim with me not to ask what, under similar circumstances, I would not grant, your majesty will do me the justice to believe that this request appears to me, to correspond with those great principles of magnanimity and wisdom, which form the basis of sound policy and durable glory."—But his imperial majesty was either destitute of the *humanity* and *magnanimity*, to which Washington appealed; or was prevented granting the request, through some promises to an *"holy alliance,"* which even then existed among the princes of Europe.

Several members of the British Parliament made an effort, at this time, for the enlargement of Lafayette and his three friends from the dungeon of Olmutz. General Fitzpatrick moved for an address to his majesty, stating "that the detention of Lafayette and others by order of the King of Prussia and Emperor of Austria, was dishonorable to the cause of the allies, and praying him to interfere for their release." In support of his motion, he remarked, that although Lafayette was imprisoned by the allied powers on the continent, yet the government of Great Britain would be implicated in the cruel act, unless it should attempt his liberation, as it had now become a member of the coalition against the anarchical conduct of the French. He contended that justice and humanity required them to intercede in behalf of this oppressed and injured man. The generous Briton insisted, that Lafayette, though a friend to civil liberty, was a firm advocate for constitutional principles, and was in favor of the power of the King as in a limited monarchy: and made a powerful appeal to the generosity and honor of his countrymen, to unite in soliciting for the freedom of Lafayette. Colonel Tarlton, then a member of Parliament, who had been opposed to Lafayette in America, in the campaign of 1781, supported the motion of his military friend; and with great eloquence, urged the propriety and justice of his liberation. Mr. Fox also spoke in favor of an address to the King, for this humane purpose. But their arguments and their eloquence were vain. It did not consist with the existing policy of the British cabinet, to listen to the proposition. The motion was lost by a large majority.

Bollman proceeded to Olmutz, and thence to Vienna, where he was so fortunate as to meet with young Huger; and they cordially united in the humane and chivalrous project of rescuing the generous Lafayette, They both repaired immediately to Olmutz, and there became acquainted with two other gentlemen, who favoured their benevolent scheme. But the difficulty of effecting it can be easily imagined. A physician of Olmutz was engaged to make known the plan to Lafayette, when he visited him in prison, then in reality, or apparently in a debilitated state of health. He had, in fact, been attacked with fever at Magdeburg, which at one time was feared would terminate his valuable life, and from the effects of which he had not fully recovered. By him a note was communicated to Lafayette, which he answered with his blood. In a short time, the physician prevailed on the governor of the city to permit his prisoner to take an airing, occasionally, in a coach, attended by a guard. It was concerted, that in one of his short excursions with the governor, he should leave the carriage under some pretence, when he was to be joined by Bollman and Huger, and immediately conducted under cover of a dark night, to the confines of Silesia, beyond the territory of the Emperor of Austria. He alighted from the carriage, near a small wood, and his generous friends, who were ready to protect him, immediately attempted to convey him away on horseback; but the guard, which accompanied the carriage, suspecting some design, pushed forward into the wood, and attempted to seize the noble prisoner, and his brave friends. A desperate struggle ensued, in which the Marquis was wounded; but they succeeded in escaping from the guard. Huger was seen and followed by some of the peasantry; and after a long pursuit was overtaken and secured. The governor and his guard returned to Olmutz; alarm guns were immediately fired, and the whole population for several miles was soon engaged in search of Lafayette and Bollman. They were taken in the course of the evening, at the distance of about ten miles from Olmutz, and conveyed back to the prison, where a most rigorous confinement awaited them. Lafayette was put in irons, and suffered the most excruciating torture. He was in a feeble state, overcome by fatigue, and suffering greatly from the bruises and wounds received in his late attempt to escape. "His anxieties, his anguish (and despair we may almost say,) at finding himself again in the power of his unrelenting jailor, so affected his nerves, that his fever returned with increased and alarming violence. In this state he was allowed nothing but a little damp and mouldy straw; irons were put round his feet, and round his waist was a chain, fastened to the wall, which barely permitted him to turn from one side to the other. No light was admitted into his cell; and he was refused even the smallest allowance of linen.

"The winter of 1794-95 was very severe, but his inhuman jailors did not relax from the rigour of prescribed and systematic oppression. It seemed, indeed as if their object was to put an end to their victim's existence by this ingenious device of incessant cruelty. Worn down by disease and the rigour of the season, his hair fell from his head, and he was emaciated to the last degree. To these physical distresses were soon super added those mental anxieties, which perhaps, were still more difficult to endure. The only information he could obtain respecting the fate of his wife and children, for whom he felt the greatest solicitude, was, that they were confided in the prisons of Paris: and in reply to his enquiries concerning his most generous friends, Bollman and Huger, he was informed by his unfeeling tormentors that they were soon to perish by the hands of the hangman."

Bollman and Huger were kept in close confinement in the prison at Olmutz, for some time, for having attempted to rescue Lafayette from his cruel imprisonment. The keepers of the prison were unfeeling men; and instead of slowing any favour to their prisoners, who ought to have received their admiration, subjected them to unnecessary severity. They were subjected to strict examination, after a long confinement, and the sentence of their judges was in favour of their liberation, on paying a large amount to government. By the aid of some generous friends, they were furnished with the requisite sums, and discharged from the prison. But Lafayette was still detained in prison, and in the same suffering and shameful condition as before mentioned. It was several months before his irons and chains were removed; which was effected through the very benevolent individuals, who had secretly favoured his recent attempt to escape; but who, happily both for him and themselves, were not suspected of any agency in the plot: these were an opulent Jewish merchant, and the chief surgeon to the prisoners. They prevailed also with the civil authority to grant permission to the Marquis to walk an hour each day, in front of the prison, though in custody of a strong guard of soldiers, and no one was allowed to speak to him.

Unutterably painful and distressing must have been the situation of Madame Lafayette ever after the fatal day, when her beloved and affectionate husband felt it his duty to depart from France, and leave her and their three children unprotected, and subject to the insults and severities of an enraged and lawless mob. She and her two daughters, then about fifteen and twelve, were cast into prison in Paris. The family estates were confiscated, and most of his particular friends fell by the stroke of the guillotine. In this agonizing condition, she maintained the most wonderful fortitude and patience; without uncommon firmness and sincere trust in providence, she must have sunk under such deep and complicated distress. While she was in prison, she was often found in a retired spot, engaged in holy and humble supplication to heaven. When she was released from the prison, after about twenty months of degrading confinement, her constitution was greatly enfeebled, and her friends and physician advised her to seek repose at some retired place in the country. But she refused, and feeble and emaciated as she was, she resolved to proceed immediately to Olmutz, and to bury herself in prison with her husband, unless she could possibly procure his liberation. With this purpose in view, she went first to Vienna, to endeavour to concilitate the favor and influence of the Emperor. Through the friendly interposition of two noble females, acquainted at court, she was admitted to an audience with the Emperor.

He received her graciously, and professed a desire that her request might be fulfilled; but gave no positive orders for the liberation of Lafayette because his *political* engagements with other courts prevented it. He, however, consented that she might visit her husband. She accordingly repaired to Olmutz, to minister, as an angel of light, to his comfort, though not clothed with power to give him that liberty, which they ardently hoped. She and her daughters shared with him the confinement of a dreary prison, for nearly two years. It was not until 1797, that they were set at liberty: and this was immediately owing to the influence of General Bonaparte, on his victories over the Austrians in that year. Lafayette expressed his gratitude for this generous interference; but he made no sacrifice of principle, and was never his admirer or supporter.

While confined in the prison of Olmutz, with her husband, Madame Lafayette, whose health was much impaired by her sorrows and suffering, requested leave to visit Vienna for a week. She was informed her request would be granted on condition, that her daughters should be kept in a separate apartment from their father, and that she herself would never again enter the prison. She declined the offer, with indignation. Her letter on the subject, concludes thus-"Whatever may be the state of my own health and the inconvenience attending the stay of my daughters in this place we will most gratefully take advantage of the goodness his imperial majesty has expressed towards us, by the *permission to share in the miseries of this captivity.*"

When the Emperor of Austria agreed to his liberation, he proposed certain conditions, to which Lafayette refused his assent. One was that he should immediately leave Europe and embark to America. "This", said the noble-minded Marquis, "has often been my desire and intention: but as my consent to this proposition, at the present moment, would be an acknowledgment of his right to impose such a condition, I cannot comply with the demand." — The other was, that as the principles which Lafayette professed were supposed to be incompatible with the safety of the Austrian government, the Emperor could not consent that he should again enter his territory without a special permission. To this Lafayette replied, "that there already existed antecedent obligations, of which he could not divest himself; partly towards America, but chiefly towards France; and that he could not engage to do any thing, which should interfere with the rights of his country to his personal services. With these exceptions, he assured the Emperor's ambassador, that it was his firm resolution not to set foot again on any part of his Majesty's dominions."

When he was set free from the long and severe incarceration at Olmutz, Lafayette proceeded to the neutral city of Hamburg, with his family; where he received the kindest and most respectful attentions from some American gentlemen, then in that place, and also from many of the distinguished citizens, who cherished the highest regard for his character, and his meritorious services in the cause of liberty. It was at this time, that his son, George Washington Lafayette, joined the family, on his return from the United States, where he had just then passed several years. After a short residence in Hamburg, Lafayette accepted the invitation of an Hanoverian nobleman, and passed some time at his elegant chateau in Holstein, where his eldest daughter was married to Latour Maubourg, a brother of one of the Marquis' staff officers, who retired with him from France, August 1792; and had shared with him the severities of the prison of Magdeburg and Olmutz. He then resided some time in the family of a French emigrant, living in that vicinity, and who was a distant relative of Madame Lafayette. In this situation he studied the agriculture of Holstein; and gave particular attention to the raising of merino sheep, an object in which he was also engaged after his return to La Grange, his country seat near Paris.

In 1800 a new revolution took place in the French government. The Directors were found to be incompetent to the support of order; cabals and factions still existed, and confusion prevailed through the nation. General Bonaparte, who had led the armies to victory in several campaigns, was ambitious of the sole direction of public affairs. The executive power, by the new constitution, was to be placed in three Consuls, of whom Napoleon was elected chief. A Conservative Senate, so called, was to constitute a part of the Legislature and to be joined with the Consuls also in providing for the public welfare in cases of particular emergency. By the constitutionalists and those opposed to the violent factions, by which France had been long agitated and disgraced, this change was considered as auspicious to the cause of rational liberty. They hoped that a more stable government would be now formed, and that their country would enjoy a season of repose. Lafayette seized this favorable moment to return to France, after an absence of nearly eight years. His patriotic feelings had not abated, though he had suffered so long and so intensely from the hatred of those who directed the destinies of his country. His love of liberty was not weakened, though many of his countrymen, with its sacred name on their lips, had committed excesses almost without a parallel in the most despotic governments. The First Consul incited Lafayette to take a seat in the Conservative Senate; but he declined; by which he gave new proofs of his disinterested and sincere attachment to the constitutional liberty and the rights of the people. After several conversations with Bonaparte, he was satisfied of the ambitious views of this military adventurer. He perceived that the constitution was to serve as an apology for the exercise of unlimited power in the First Consul; and that representatives and senators were to be the humble ministers of his will. He saw that the constitution did not emanate from the will of the people; and was not calculated to secure and promote their welfare. Bonaparte also had discernment to learn, that Lafayette was too sincere a friend to civil liberty and to the interests of the people, to support his purposes, or to submit to his plans of personal aggrandizement.

We shall have a more just estimation of the noble sentiments with which Lafayette was animated, in declining the generous offers of the First Consul, when it is considered, that, in addition to his self-banishment to private life, he also refused an honorable salary of 7000 dollars, when the estates which remained in his possession yielded only 2000 dollars. He had a grant of land from the American Congress, in consideration of his important services in the revolution, estimated to be worth 100,000 dollars. Before the revolution, his income was 50,000 dollars: but the most valuable of his patrimonial property, as well as that which accrued to him in consequence of his marriage, had been seized by the lawless robbers of the revolution.

It was in conformity to the principles, which he had long professed and by which he was constantly guided, that he soon after opposed the election of Bonaparte as Consul for life. He would have consented, perhaps, to the claims of the aspiring Napoleon to be the First Magistrate of France, under a constitution, which expressly defined and restricted his power, and at the same time provided a sufficient guaranty of the liberties of the people.

On this occasion he wrote thus to the First Consul — "When a man, who is deeply impressed with a sense of the gratitude he owes you, and who is too ardent a lover of glory to be indifferent to yours, connects his suffrage with conditional restrictions, those restrictions not only secure him from suspicion, but prove amply, that no one will more gladly than himself behold in you the chief magistrate for life, of a free and independent republic.

"The eighteenth Brumaire saved France from destruction and I felt myself reassured and recalled by the liberal declarations to which you have connected the sanction of your honor. In your consular authority there was afterwards discerned that salutary dictatorial prerogative, which under the auspices of a genius like yours, accomplished such glorious purposes — yet less glorious, let me add, than the restoration of liberty would prove.

"It is not possible, general, that you, the first among that order of mankind, which surveys every age and every country, can desire that a revolution, marked by an unexampled series of stupendous victories and unheard of sufferings, shall give nothing to the world but a renovated system of arbitrary government. The people of this country have been acquainted with their rights too long, to forget them forever: but perhaps they may recover and enjoy them better now than during the period of revolutionary effervescence. And you, by the strength of your character and the influence of public confidence, by the superiority of your talents, your power, and your fortunes, in re-establishing the liberties of France, can allay all agitations, calm all anxieties and subdue all dangers.

"When I wish, then, to see the career of your glory crowned by the honors of perpetual magistracy, I but act in correspondence with my own private sentiments, and am influenced exclusively by patriotic considerations. But all my political and moral obligations, the principles which have governed every action of my life, call on me to pause before I bestow on you my suffrage, until I feel assured that your authority shall be erected on a basis worthy of the nation and yourself.

"I confidently trust, general, that you will recognize here, as you have done on all other occasions, a steady continuance of my political opinions, combined with the sincerest prayers for your welfare, and the deepest sense of all my obligations towards you."

Here closed all connexion between Lafayette and Bonaparte. The First Consul not only avoided all intercourse with one so sincerely devoted to the cause of liberty; but he treated him with that studied neglect, which was little short of persecution. There was indeed nothing congenial either in the character or principles of these two distinguished men. The one was aiming at power by any means, without regard to the rights or happiness of his fellow men; the other was anxious for the permanent establishment of a mild government in his native country, for the true welfare and liberty of the people; and was willing to make every sacrifice for the attainment of such great objects.

The unfriendly feelings of Bonaparte were extended even to the younger Lafayette. This patriotic youth, with much of the public spirit of his noble father, engaged in the service of his country soon after his return from America. He was an aid of the brave Grouchy, general of division; an active, intelligent, meritorious officer, and distinguished on various occasions. But he received neither advancement nor distinction from the Emperor. It was, on the contrary, the wish of Napoleon, that young Lafayette would send in his resignation, and retire from the army. When this was made known to him, he observed, "that as long as his country was involved in war, he should not disgrace himself by a resignation; and that he should be ashamed to think of it, while his companions were daily exposing themselves to danger. It was true, he was an American citizen, but he was first of all a Frenchman and a loyal Frenchman."

G. W. Lafayette was much esteemed by the officers who knew him, of all ranks; and they frequently solicited his promotion; but the Emperor disregarded alike the merits of the youthful hero and the entreaties of his military friends. He continued in the army until the treaty of Tilsit.

To a man of his great sensibility and warmth of affection, the severest affliction which Lafayette has been called to endure, great and various as have been his sufferings, now awaited him. His amiable, his attached and devoted wife was torn from him, in his retreat, within a few years after his return to France; when he more than ever, perhaps, needed her company and solace, to fortify his mind under the multiplied disappointments from the world.

She had never enjoyed perfect health after her imprisonment at Olmutz. But possessed of uncommon fortitude and imbued with religious sentiments, she was still instrumental in promoting the happiness of her husband and family. Her patience, her equanimity, her sweetness of temper never forsook her. But her constitution was broken, and a sudden paralysis deprived her of her physical strength and almost of speech. At the urgent request of her husband, though with reluctance, she was conveyed to Paris for medical assistance; but it proved in vain. She died in December 1807.

While Madame de Lafayette was in the prison in Paris, though treated with the greatest severity by Robespierre and his party, she had the consolation of sharing in the sympathetic kindness and assistance of many individuals, who were willing to expose themselves to the hatred of her cruel persecutors for her relief. A gentleman from Boston, Joseph Russel, Esq. then a resident in Paris, made great efforts for her liberation; although by this generous interference he hazarded his own life. It was through his friendly assistance, that her son G. W. Lafayette, then about fourteen years of age, was conveyed to the United States, where he remained till the discharge of his parents from the dungeons of Olmutz.

About this period, and soon after the death of his amiable wife, General Lafayette received a severe fracture in one of his legs, by a fall, which occasioned his confinement for nearly twelve months, and was the cause of his present lameness. He had been transacting business with the minister of the marine; and in going from the office to his carriage, a distance of two hundred paces, late in the evening, after a heavy rain and sleet, which had rendered it dangerous walking, he fell suddenly and broke a bone.

For six or seven years, till 1814, when Louis XVIII. returned to France to mount the throne of the Bourbons, Lafayette resided at his chateau of La Grange, an inactive spectator of the political changes which took place. No doubt he had a sufficient apology for this inaction and voluntary retreat from public affairs. He was too honest and too candid, too much an enemy to the anarchy of the jacobin factions, and to the despotism of the Emperor, to support either, or to be received into their confidence. He would probably have been satisfied with the restoration of a Bourbon to the throne, if the throne could be founded in a constitution, admitting the representatives of the people to a share in legislation, and defining the extent and the measure of the executive authority. He was animated by the same principles and sentiments which governed him in the part he acted in 1789 and 1792: and although he might acquiesce in a different government, either under the First Consul, or under Louis XVIII. he could not, consistently, and therefore he chose not to forward their views by his own personal influence and support. He was still calumniated by some agents of the Bourbons, yet he declared, on the return of Bonaparte from Elba, to gain the throne of France, "that in all measures, which should promote or be consistent with the liberties of the people, he would aid the cause of the legitimate heir of the crown." The views of Louis' friends and allies were too arbitrary to lead them to expect his approbation and aid.

Louis XVIII. had not been long in France, before great discontent was manifested among the citizens at the prospect of his being placed on the throne of his brother. Napoleon and his friends took advantage of this state of things: he left his retreat in the Island of Elba, and returned to Paris. Louis was obliged to retire. Bonaparte, through his brother Joseph, the ex-king of Spain, solicited of Lafayette to accept of a peerage. But he promptly declined; but observed, "that if there should be a convocation of a chamber of representatives," which he strenuously urged, "he would consent to take a part in public affairs, should he be elected." His independence and his want of faith in Napoleon, were preserved, notwithstanding the urgent advances of the latter; and he resolutely refused to go near him till after his final abdication. Yet even at this time, Lafayette thought he might rely on "his cordial opposition to all foreign invasion and influence, and to any family or party which should avail itself of such assistance in order to attack the independence and the liberties of France." Much as he distrusted the views of Bonaparte, and desirous as he was of some explicit guaranty, from him and his supporters, for the liberty of the French people, he would not unite with the Bourbons, who were resolved to place Louis XVIII. firmly on the throne of his ancestors, by any means in their power, and who had collected an army of one million two hundred thousand foreigners to accomplish their object, at the risque of a civil war, and a general slaughter, similar to that with which the unprincipled, revolutionary Jacobins had before afflicted the nation.

Lafayette was now elected a member of the chamber of deputies from his own department, though he had protested against the articles of the constitution of the empire, and of the additional act which conspired against the *sovereignty* of the people, and the rights of the citizens. This was a strong proof of the sense the people had of his integrity and his patriotism. After the battle of Waterloo, Napoleon returned to Paris, in consternation, and undecided as to the course he would pursue on this signal reverse of fortune. Some of his friends advised him again to abdicate the office of Emperor, which he held by so precarious a tenure; others suggested decisive and bold measures, with a view to fortify himself in power, even in apposition to the will and wishes of the deputies. He attempted to prorogue the chamber of representatives, and have himself proclaimed perpetual dictator. Lafayette was then present in the chamber; and with his usual independence and energy, made the following observations.

"When, for the first time for many years, I raise my voice; which the old friends of liberty will recognise again, I feel constrained to address you, gentlemen, on the imminent danger of the country, which you alone are able to prevent.

"Disastrous reports have been circulated and are now unhappily confirmed. Now is the time to rally round the old tri-coloured standard of 1789, of liberty, of equality, and of public order. It is this alone which we are bound to defend against foreign pretensions and domestic factions. Allow a veteran in this holy cause, who has always been an enemy to the baneful spirit of dissension, to submit the following preliminary resolutions" of which I hope you will admit the necessity.

"*First*. The Chamber of Representatives declare that the independence of the nation is endangered.

"*Second*. The Chamber declare themselves in continued session— That every attempt to prorogue the Chamber shall be considered high treason—That any one guilty of such an attempt shall be deemed a traitor to his country, and be instantly proceeded against as such.

"*Third*. The army of the line and the national guards, who have fought and are still fighting for the independence of France, deserve the gratitude of their Country.

"*Fourth*. The minister of the interior is directed to assemble the general staff, the commandants and majors of the legion of the national guard of Paris, to consult on the means of supplying them with arms, and to render complete this citizen-guard; whose zeal and patriotism having been proved for twenty-six years, offer a sure guaranty of the liberty, the property and the tranquility of the capital, and of the inviolability of the representatives of the nation.

"*Fifth*. The ministers of war, of foreign relations, of the interior and of the police, are invited to attend the assembly immediately."

When the Emperor was informed that Lafayette was in the tribune, and engaged in the discussions on the proposition of constituting him dictator for life, he expressed great alarm and anxiety. He knew the sentiments of Lafayette too well, not to feel assured of his opposition to such a measure. For this consistent and zealous advocate for the rights of the people had always been hostile to a chief magistrate, under any title, who should possess absolute power; and contended for a constitution to limit and define the executive authority. It was then that. Bonaparte exclaimed, "Lafayette in the tribune!" and his great agitation betrayed the belief, that his power was at an end. In this situation, his armies defeated, and the representatives of the people opposed to his wishes of a *perpetual* dictatorship, he gave formal notice of his purpose to abdicate the imperial authority. Lafayette was at the head of the deputation appointed by the chamber of representatives, to wait on the Emperor, to accept and thank him for his abdication, A few days before this, when the deputies were accused of being capricious and ungrateful, by a friend of Napoleon, Lafayette observed, in reply, "go tell him that we can trust him no longer; we ourselves will undertake the salvation of our country."

Although he opposed the ambitious views of Bonaparte, and boldly and decidedly remonstrated against his intention of again assuming absolute power, yet he moved in the chamber of Representatives, at this time, that the liberty and person of the late Emperor Napoleon should be placed under the protection of the French nation; expecting, probably, that the allied princes of Europe, already in the vicinity of Paris with powerful armies, would take his life, or cause him to be imprisoned.

Lafayette was one of the Commissioners appointed by the Chamber of Deputies to propose to the allied powers a suspension of hostilities. His object was to provide for the liberty of the people and to exact a promise of some limitations and restrictions to the royal authority. But the friends and supporters of the Bourbon dynasty, the hereditary princes of Europe, had a powerful army in the suburbs of Paris, and they refused to make any terms with the most moderate and honorable advocates of popular rights. Though one tyrant was overthrown; another was to be *forced* upon them: not precisely an usurper indeed; but who, without a constitution for his guide, and surrounded by men of arbitrary principles might be instrumental in their oppression and degradation. When he returned to Paris, he found the invading armies in possession of the city. Napoleon escaped, and *nominal* tranquility was restored to the capital of France. But it was a tranquility produced by a military force; and not that which is the effect of a wise and energetic government founded in the will of the people. The doors of the assembly were closed against the representatives of the people, by the *gens d'armes*, the agents who restored the Bourbon dynasty. Many of the deputies then assembled at the house of Lafayette; at whose instance they repaired to the President's to record their testimony to this forced and unjust exclusion, and to sign the *proces verbal.*

As he alike disapproved of Louis or Napoleon assuming the power of King or Emperor, without a bill of rights securing the privileges of the people, and a constitution as the rule and measure of executive acts, it was no longer in his power to render service to his country is a public station: nor did the favorites of Louis XVIII. invite him to take part in the administration of government, which they proposed to establish. It may appear surprising, on the first view of the subject, that the friends of a monarch of the reputed mild character of Louis, who must wish the greatest happiness of his subjects, should refuse to such men as Lafayette, all share in the government; and at the same time, take into their employment and confidence, many of the creatures of Bonaparte, who were destitute alike of principle and patriotism. But it is often found to be the fact, that the sincere and honest, who will not flatter, and do not approve all the projects of an ambitious aspirant, or an arbitrary Prince, are less courted, than those who have no settled principles, or one ever ready to support the successful candidate for power.

Except the short and occasional engagements in political concerns, just above related, Lafayette, after his return to France in the year 1800, generally remained at his estate, about thirty miles from Paris. But though retired from the more active scenes of public life, he enjoyed the friendship of several eminent characters in his own country; and was visited by all distinguished Americans, and many British statesmen and scholars, whose business or amusement led them to travel through France. He was always particularly desirous to learn the affairs of America, his adopted country; and was careful to procure all the publications from the United States. Besides literary pursuits, he was occasionally occupied in attending to the cultivation and improvement of his family estate. Such has frequently been the employment and solace of eminent men, when they have retired from high public stations, in which their services and exactions have met the mistaken censure or the neglect of the world. During several of the first years of this retirement, he was blessed with the society of an amiable and affectionate wife. And after her much lamented death, which has been before noticed, he still enjoyed the pleasure of being surrounded by his children and grand children, in whose education and improvement he always took a truly paternal interest.

At the time the federal constitution was in discussion by conventions in the several states, and when it first went into operation, Alexander Hamilton, who was its zealous advocate, corresponded with Lafayette on the subject. The letters have not been published; but it is probable they would be highly interesting to the politician and statesman, and serve fully to develop the views of both these eminent men on the science of civil government. This was about the period of the commencement of the French revolution. The particular extent of the change in the monarchical government of France, contemplated by Lafayette, may appear by this epistolary discussion. If not wholly confidential, it may be expected, that the letters will be given to the American public.

His second daughter, Virginia, married Monsieur de Lasteyrie, a young gentleman of eminent literary attainments; and who distinguished himself, also, as an officer in the French army, during the reign of Napoleon; particularly in the campaign of Jena, Eylau, Friedland, &c. But this brave and meritorious officer shared, with his brother-in-law, G. W. Fayette, the constant neglect and hatred of Bonaparte. G. W. Fayette was married to a daughter of Count de Tracy, one of the party of moderates, or liberals, as often denominated, and sometime a member of the conservative senate. The son and sons-in-law of General Lafayette, reside at the same chateau with their father; which is sufficiently spacious, not only for the respectable accommodation of the four united families, the father, son and two sons-in-law; but for the reception and occasional residence of family or other particular friends, who often pass much time in this hospitable mansion. Monsieur de Maubourg, an old and intimate friend of General Lafayette, with his lady, usually spend the greater part of the year at the chateau of La Grange. The son, and eldest daughter, who married Charles Latour Maubourg, have each several children, who are peculiar objects of affection and interest with their respected grandsire:

The following remarks of Madame de Stael, who personally knew much of General Lafayette, [Footnote: She was also an intimate friend of Madame de Lafayette. They were accused, in the days of suspicion and terror, of being too much engaged in political affairs.] and who was well acquainted with characters and events connected with the French revolution, are deemed worthy of being presented to the reader of these hasty memoirs.

"M. de Lafayette, having fought from his early youth for the cause of America, had early become imbued with the principles of liberty, which form the basis of that government. If he made mistakes with regard to the French revolution, we are to ascribe them all to his admiration of the American institutions, and of Washington, the hero citizen, who guided the first steps of that nation in the career of Independence. Lafayette, young, affluent, of noble family, and beloved at home, relinquished all these advantages at the age of nineteen, to serve beyond the ocean in the cause of that liberty, the love of which has decided every action of his life. Had he had the happiness to be a native of the United States, his conduct would have been that of Washington: the same disinterestedness, the same enthusiasm, the same perseverance in their opinions, distinguished each of these generous friends of humanity. Had General Washington been, like the Marquis de Lafayette, commander of the national guard of Paris, he also might have found it impossible to control the course of circumstances; *he* also might have seen his efforts baffled by the difficulty of being at once faithful to his engagements to the king, and of establishing at the same time, the liberty of his country.

"M. de Lafayette, I must say, has a right to be considered a true republican: none of the vanities of his rank, ever entered his head: power, the effect of which is so great in France, had no ascendancy over him: the desire of pleasing in a drawing room conversation, did not with him influence a single phrase: he sacrificed all his fortune to his opinions, with the most generous indifference. When in the prisons of Olmutz, as when at the height of his influence, he was equally firm in his attachment to his principles. His manner of seeing and acting, is open and direct. Whoever has marked his conduct, may foretell with certainty what he will do on any particular occasion. His political feeling is that of a citizen of the United States; and even his person is more English than French. The hatred, of which M. de Lafayette is the object, has never embittered his temper; and his gentleness of soul is complete: at the same time nothing has ever modified his opinions; and his confidence in the triumph of liberty, is the same as that of a pious man in a future life. These sentiments, so contrary to the selfish calculations of most of the men who have acted a part in France, may appear pitiable in the eyes of some persons—"it is so silly" they think, "to prefer one's country to one's self; not to change one's party when that party is worsted; in short, to consider mankind, not as cards with which to play a winning game, but as the sacred objects of unlimited sacrifices." If this is to form the charge of silliness, would that it were but once merited by our men of talents!

"It is a singular phenomenon, that such a character as that of M. de Lafayette, should have appeared in the foremost rank of the French *noblesse*; but he can neither be censured nor exculpated with impartiality, without being acknowledged to be such as I have described him. It then becomes easy to understand the different contrasts which naturally arose between his disposition and situation. Supporting monarchy more from duty than attachment, he drew involuntarily towards the principles of the democrats, whom he was obliged to resist; and a certain kindness for the advocates of the republican form, was perceptible in him, although his reflection forbade the admission of their system into France. Since the departure of M. de Lafayette for America, now forty years ago, we cannot quote a single action or a single word of his, which was not direct and consistent. Personal interest never blended itself in the least with his public conduct: success would have displayed such sentiments to advantage; but they claim the attention of the historian in spite of circumstances, and in spite of faults, which may serve as a handle to his opponents."

M. Lafayette was returned a member of the chamber of deputies from his own department, in 1819, though his election was opposed by the ministerial party. Some members rejoiced to see again among them, the "friend and disciple of Washington;" while others, the adherents of monarchy, viewed him with distrust and jealousy, as "the veteran general of the revolution." He was not a very active member of this legislative body; for he was convinced it would be in vain to attempt restoring the constitution of 1789. He seldom attended the assembly: but on several questions, when he was present, discovered the same political sentiments which directed his conduct in the early days of the revolution. The minister offered a proposition for establishing a censorship over the public journals, and for arresting persons suspected of being inimical to the restoration of the Bourbons. Lafayette spoke against the proposed law, "as subversive of all order, of all right, and of the natural and just privileges of the citizens." He referred to the evils consequent upon all arbitrary proceedings against persons merely suspected of being unfriendly to the government, and to the probable mischiefs which would arise from a severe restriction upon the liberty of the press. The minister himself acknowledged, that the proposition was not wholly consistent with the national rights of the citizens; but insisted upon its expediency in the present state of the nation. At this time, also, he reminded the ministers of promises, which had been made by the political friends of Louis XVIII. in favor of the liberties of the people. He "conjured them to maintain the liberties of France, within the limits prescribed by the constitution." "To violate it," said he, "is to dissolve the mutual guarantees of the nation and of the throne; it is to give ourselves up to a total primitive freedom from all duties and all laws." This discussion was unusually animated, and Lafayette was very decided in his opposition to the measure. The course pursued by the court was condemned, and some severity of remark was indulged in, as to the designs of ministers. The ministerial party obtained but a small majority in favor of the law; and some fermentation was excited in Paris in relation to this subject. The *liberals*, or the friends of constitutional freedom, were insulted, and the life of Lafayette was openly menaced.

This year, a society was formed among the friends of constitutional freedom, for the relief of those, who were arrested on mere suspicion, or on a charge of violating the restrictions on the press; but who were believed to be unjustly suspected, and who had been found entirely innocent, even in the eye of the law, rigid as were its provisions. This was a numerous society; consisting of fifty four members of the chamber of deputies, and many other opulent and literary citizens; at the head of which we find the name of M. Lafayette.

The distinguished Americans and Englishmen who have visited Lafayette, at his family mansion of La Grange, describe his residence and its inmates as most beautiful and interesting. "It is situated in the fertile district of La Brie, thirty miles from Paris, remote from any common road, and far distant from the bustling world. In the midst of a luxuriant wilderness, rising above prolific orchards and antiquated woods, appears the five towers of La Grange, tinged with the golden rays of the declining sun. The deep moat, the draw bridge; the ivied tower and arched portals, opening into a large square court, has a feudal and picturesque character; and the associations which occur, on entering the residence of a man so heroic, so disinterested, so celebrated, fill the mind with peculiar admiration, and excite the most lively interest." The family party, partaking more of patriarchal than of courtly manners, is composed of individuals mutually attached, and anxious only for mutual improvement and happiness. It represents the younger members, as employed in their studies or engaged in innocent recreations so salutary to the youthful temper and constitution: and the older, as occupied in useful and literary pursuits, or devoted to the more enlivening pleasures of conversation.

"The venerable head of this happy family, at the age of sixty seven, is in the full possession of every talent and faculty. His memory has all the tenacity of youthful recollection. On his person, time has yet made little visible impression. Not a wrinkle furrows the ample brow; and his unbent and noble figure is still as upright, bold and vigorous, as the mind which informs it. Grace, strength and dignity still distinguish the fine person of this extraordinary man; who, though more than forty years before the world, engaged in scenes of strange and eventful conflict, does not yet appear to have reached his grand climactic. Active on his farm; graceful and elegant in his *salon*, it is difficult to trace, in one of the most successful agriculturists, and one of the most perfect fine gentlemen of France, a warrior and a legislator. But the patriot is always discernible. His conversation is enriched with anecdotes of all that is celebrated in character or event, for the last fifty years. His elegant and well chosen collection of books, occupies the highest apartments in one of the towers of the chateau; and, like the study of Montaigne, hangs over the farm yard of the philosophical agriculturist. It frequently happens, said M. Lafayette, to one of his visitors as they were looking from a window on some flocks, which were moving beneath, that my merinos and my hay carts dispute my attention to Hume or Voltaire."

Of the benevolent affections of Lafayette, his whole life affords abundant proofs. He was possessed of the most patriotic and generous feeling. Numerous instances are also related of his kindness to individuals, and of his private benefactions. The children of his tenants, and neighbours were objects of his generosity and complacency. And those who are unjustly oppressed or defrauded, were sure to find in him, an able advocate. The widow of an American officer, of French parentage, who was left destitute at the death of her gallant husband, had a claim for patrimonial estates in France. The legal evidence to substantiate her claim was exceedingly difficult to be procured. The case was made known to Lafayette, and he never ceased his exertions until he recovered the greater part of the estate.

Soon after the arrival of young Lafayette in Boston, 1795, he wrote to General Washington, then President of the United States, informing him of his situation, and requesting advice and counsel from the friend of his father. As the chief magistrate of the nation, it would not have been prudent in Washington, publicly to interfere in his behalf—Lafayette, at this period, was almost equally obnoxious to the rulers of France, as any one of the royal family. He had, indeed, been most *unjustly* denounced and proscribed by the dominant party; but they pretended he was attached to a monarchy; and a public official act of patronage in the President, towards young Lafayette, would have furnished a pretext for complaint against the government. Washington had already given proof, that he did not approve of the conduct of the French Directory, nor of the proceedings of their minister in America. But though a prudent policy forbid all official attention and aid to the son of Lafayette the generous & noble feelings of Washington induced him to give assurances of personal regard, and of a readiness to afford all proper assistance towards the education and support of this youthful subject of political persecution. He wrote to his friend, Hon. George Cabot, stating the reasons for declining to act officially or publicly in the case; but requesting Mr. C. to assure young Lafayette that he might consider him as a father, a friend and protector. Washington expressed a desire in this letter, that he should become a member of the university in Cambridge, if qualified for admission, where he would be under the inspection and tuition of excellent men; for he was aware that want of employment would lead to dissipation; and that the season of youth was to be diligently improved for the cultivation of the mind. He desired Mr. C. to call on him to meet any expenses which might accrue in his education and support. The French tutor, who attended young Lafayette, chose to have him under his own private instruction; and he did not enter the university. The kindness and generosity of Washington were not the less meritorious in the appeal made to him by the son of his own, and of his country's friend.

Among the many eminent characters by whom General Lafayette was visited in his retirement at La Grange, after his return to France, (in 1800) was CHARLES J. FOX, the celebrated British statesman. The family of Mr. Fox, for several generations, was ranked among the whip party in England, and firm friends of the glorious revolution of 1689; when the House of Stuart was excluded from the throne, and William and Mary acknowledged as the legitimate sovereigns. Mr. Fox was of the same political school with the elder PITT, whose powerful talents were successfully exerted for the glory of Great Britain, in the latter part of the reign of George II. and who was a firm and decided advocate for the rights of the British colonies in 1775. When Lafayette and family were confined in the dungeons at Olmutz, Mr. Fox, with others, then members of the British Parliament, pleaded the cause of these unhappy sufferers, with great eloquence, but without effect. He had been personally acquainted with the celebrated French philanthropist, before this period; and was attached to his character and principles, as a zealous friend of civil liberty. The interview between these two highly distinguished reformers is represented to have been peculiarly interesting. Perhaps, the plans of reform proposed by Mr. Fox, could not have been carried into effect, at that time, without danger to the stability of the British government; but the general character of Fox, gave evidence of the sincerity of his upright purposes; and of the purity of the motives by which Lafayette was actuated, in the course he pursued in France, in 1789, and subsequently, cannot be justly doubted, though the revolution did not result in the, political benefits be had anticipated.

When Mr. Fox was in Paris, some time in 1802, Lafayette hastened from his retired residence, at La Grange, to call on him. The writer, who gives an account of this meeting, observes, "that a stranger of an interesting and graceful figure, came gently in," where he and Mr. Fox were sitting, at the hotel in Paris, "advanced rapidly; and, embracing Mr. Fox, showed a countenance full of joy, while tears rolled down his cheeks; Mr. Fox testified equal emotion. It was M. de Lafayette, the virtuous and unshaken friend of liberty. He had come from the country to see Mr. Fox, and to invite him to his house. In a few moments their sentiments were interchanged. The review of the past was taken in a moment; and they soon appeared to be affectionate friends, who having parted for a few days, were now reunited. Lafayette viewed the new state of things with regret; not from any personal dislike of the first consul, but from a rooted and principled conviction, that arbitrary power is injurious to the happiness of mankind.

"In his retirement, and filled with gloomy prospects of the republic, he lived in the most private and simple manner. In the bosom of an amiable and affectionate family, he found every consolation. He frequented no place of amusement; and, with a very limited fortune, exhibited the bright example of a public man, content with a little, free from all envious and angry feelings: and willing to live in dignified silence, when he had not the power or influence to do good."

The visit of Mr. Fox and his friend to La Grange, is thus described—"The towers and wood of the chateau appeared in peaceful repose, as we drove near; and when we gained a full view of the building, I felt great emotion; it was the residence of a great and good man—a patriot and friend of mankind, whose life had been consecrated to virtue and liberty; the family came to the hall to meet us, happy in themselves, and rejoicing to see the illustrious friend of Lafayette! I cannot forget that moment—no silly affectation, no airs of idle ceremony were seen at the residence of him, who had gloriously struggled for America, and had done all he could for France.

"M. de Lafayette and Madame received Mr. and Mrs. Fox with the heartiest welcome. The family consisted of two daughters, and a son and his wife, all young and elegant; all living with M. de Lafayette, as a brother and friend. His graceful and manly form, his benevolent countenance, his frank and warm manners, which made him almost adored by his family, and a placid contentedness, nearly allied to cheerfulness; altogether had an irresistible effect, in gaining the affections and esteem of those admitted to his more intimate society.

"Madame de Lafayette, of the noble family of Noailes, was a superior and admirable woman, possessing the high polish of the ancient nobility, eloquent and animated. Fondly attached to M. de Lafayette and her family, she regretted nothing of past splendor; she possessed an affectionate husband, and was happy in retirement. The son was a pleasing young man, and his wife engaging and interesting; the daughters were charming women, entirely free from the insipid languor or wretched affectation, which in young ladies of fashion so much destroys originality of character, and makes us find, in one of the fashionables, the prototype and pattern of thousands. In a word, this amiable and happy family seemed united by one bond of affection, and to desire nothing beyond the circle of their own tranquil mansion.

"The chateau and estate of La Grange, which Madame, who was an heiress, had brought with her, was all that remained of his fortune. He had lost every thing besides in the madness of revolutionary confiscation; and had not yet been able to procure restitution or compensation. To add to the interest of the scene, General Fitzpatrick who had known Lafayette in America, and had vainly attempted, in the British house of Commons, to rouse the ministry to a sense of humanity and justice for him, joined the party at La Grange, at this time. That accomplished man was an addition to our society, and was received most affectionately by the family of Lafayette. I have often contemplated with great pleasure, Mr. Fox, General Fitzpatrick and M. de Lafayette walking in the long shady grove near the chateau, speaking of past times, the war in America, and the revolution in France. The rare sight of three such characters was grateful to any one who felt friendly to the cause of civil liberty, and valued men for their services to humanity, rather than for successful ambition.

"Lafayette spoke a good deal of America; and we learnt from him something of his various and useful services for that country, at the court of Louis, as well as of his personal efforts, during the struggle for independence. His political career in France had not the same happy result, as in America; but it should be considered, that his situation in the former was arduous beyond measure. A friend to limited monarchy, and to the legitimate rights of the people, at a time when the support of one was deemed hostility to the other, he found it impossible, consistent with his principles, to follow the mania of the nation. A king of integrity and firmness, with Lafayette as his counselor, might have been safe, even in the tumultuous times preceding the seizure of civil power by sanguinary demagogues. But Louis, it is feared, wanted both these qualities; certainly the latter. Lafayette failed, therefore, in his patriotic views; not as Bonaparte is said to have insinuated, because he aimed at what was impracticable; but because those whose interest it was to second his views, did not support him. A ruined throne and desolate country subsequently attested the purity of his principles, and the soundness of his judgment."

General Lafayette is of the *Catholic* religion, which has been long established, and is still generally professed, in France. But he discovers nothing of that exclusive and intolerant spirit which has distinguished the church of Rome, more especially in ages past. He took an active part in favor of the proposition, in 1789, for securing the rights of conscience and the privileges of worship to the protestants of France, according to, their own particular belief. It was not to be supposed that one of his enlightened views, and knowledge of human nature, would be a bigot in religion; or would attach undue importance to the external forms and the mere ceremonies of worship. He is not, however, to be classed with many learned men in Roman Catholic countries, in modern times, who merely *profess* the papal system because it is the religion of the state, while they are real infidels; or skeptical as to the essential doctrines of christianity. It is not improbable that his intercourse with liberal and candid yet pious men is America, in his early years, served to produce in his mind charitable sentiments toward those who were educated in a system differing somewhat from that which he had been taught to revere, in its ceremonies and even in some of its dogmas. He was several years intimately acquainted with Washington, Lincoln and other military characters, who were men of sincere, though of unostentatious piety; as well as with many of the clergy of our country, whom he could not but esteem and respect; and the natural effect of such intercourse would be a liberality of opinion on religious subjects. It is, indeed, a consideration, creditable, in some measure, to those who admit it, and tending also to prove that christianity is calculated and designed to be an universal religion, that intelligent men of different countries and sects unite in receiving all the essential and practical doctrines of revelation. In a word, "that God is no respecter of persons; but that in every nation he who *feareth* him and *worketh righteousness* is accepted of him."

Having followed Lafayette through many years of an active and eventful life, and having witnessed his course in various critical and responsible situations, we may be prepared to form a correct estimate of his talents, his wisdom and his virtues. It is far from our wishes to pronounce an unqualified or exaggerated panegyric on his character. But for the honor of our species and in justice to this eminent philanthropist, it is proper that his heroic and generous actions, and his firmness and perseverance of purpose in the cause of civil liberty and of the rights of mankind, should be duly appreciated. And when we reflect upon the ardour and constancy of his efforts in favour of American Independence; upon his personal sacrifices and exposure to danger in our behalf, in the field, and his solicitations as our advocate at the court of Louis; upon his warm attachment to Washington, and to the other patriots and heroes of our glorious revolution; upon his attempts afterwards to improve the government of his own country and to place some check upon the despotic power of a selfish, calculating ministry; upon his uniform resolute, and fearless opposition to the wild projects of factious men, who obtained ephemeral influence in France, but whose conduct was equally hostile to the rights and welfare of the people as that of the agents of an absolute monarch; upon his steady and firm support of the constitution, formed by the deputies of the people, and designed to guarantee their liberties; upon his desire to support the dignity of the monarch, in unison with the rights of the citizens, and his wishes to afford security to the person of Louis; and upon his efforts to restore related and constitutional liberty, at the time the present king returned to France, and when Napoleon was aiming at unlimited power as perpetual dictator, are we not obliged to acknowledge, that few men; very few, indeed, have done so much for the social happiness of their fellows; that very few deserve the gratitude and applause, which may be justly claimed for this very eminent asserter of the rights of man. Success is too often made the criterion of human merit. It is matter of great congratulation, that our revolutionary struggle was successful; and it is believed, that Lafayette, by his influence in France, and his personal exertions here, contributed very much to its happy termination. In his own country, afterwards, he was not so fortunate in attaining and securing the object at which he aimed. But to the accurate and deep observer of character and events, it will probably be apparent, that no one, however resolute, could have established a government in France in 1790, upon the just recognition of the rights of man, and the exercise of power, (even limited power) in the reigning Prince. That Lafayette was upright and disinterested in his purpose, perhaps, no candid impartial man will deny; that any one could have produced a more fortunate issue, is at least very doubtful. He did not want decision, or energy. He often acted with great promptness, and gave proof of ready mental resources. He was also brave, and fearless of personal danger. Other men might have conducted with more energy; but it would have been at the hazard of a thousand lives and in violation of constitutional principles. That Lafayette was not more efficient, or more despotic, when he commanded the national guards, and the populace of Paris went to Versailles and insulted the royal family; or when the Jacobin faction, in June 1792, were ready to denounce him and to prostrate the constitution, did not argue want of energy but the influence of principle and a salutary love of order.

When it is recollected what important and disinterested services the Marquis de Lafayette had performed for America, in the most critical periods of our revolutionary war, and how active and uniform he had been, through all the changes and excesses in his own country for upwards of thirty years, it cannot be thought unreasonable, that the citizens of the United States held his character in high estimation, and were desirous of greeting him once more, on their own territory, which he had assisted by his zeal and valour to defend. In his letters to his friends here, and in the interviews, which he had with American gentleman at his own hospitable mansion, he frequently expressed a wish and an intention of again visiting this favored land of liberty. He cherished precious recollections of the times, long since past, when he joined with many brave and honorable spirits in the sacred cause of freedom. To the patriots and heroes who achieved our independence, he had a most sincere and cordial attachment; and his military associates who survived, and their children, who had often heard of his heroic and generous deeds, were eager on their part to welcome him to their country and their affections; and to show to him and to the world, that they entertained a high sense of his sacrifices and efforts in securing to them the privileges and blessings they so richly enjoy.

The feelings of General Lafayette will appear by the letters he wrote to his friends in this country, when he was expecting to make his long-intended visit. The following is an extract from one addressed to an old revolutionary friend, who had previously written to Lafayette. "I am deeply affected by your kindly remembrance. No one among the survivors, who sharedin our glorious cause and military fraternity, can be attached more than I am, to the memory of our departed brethren, and to the ties which bind together the surviving American companions in arm. Since our youthful revolutionary times, many vicissitudes have passed over our heads. But in every situation, I have enjoyed, with great delight, the recollection of our struggle so glorious and so pure; of our Columbian country, so excellent and promising; of our brotherly army, so gallant, so virtuous and so united. How happy for us to see the present prosperous result of the contest, which our toils and our blood have shared the honor to support."

In January 1824, when it was known, that General Lafayette proposed to take passage for the United States, the Representatives of the nation, in Congress assembled, requested the President "to offer him a public ship for his accommodation; [he declined this offer, and chose to embark in a private vessel;] and to assure him, in the name of the people of this great Republic, that they cherished for him a grateful and affectionate attachment."

The Legislature of Massachusetts also, at its session in June last, adopted a resolve, "requesting the Governor to make such arrangements, as would secure to this distinguished friend of our country, an honorable reception, on the part of this State, and authorising him to draw any sum from the public treasury to meet the expenses arising thereupon."

The Society of Cincinnati of Massachusetts, at their anniversary meeting on the fourth of July, it being then expected that General Lafayette would soon visit the United States, unanimously passed the following vote. "It being reported, that General Lafayette, an original member of the Society of Cincinnati, intends visiting the United States in the course of the present year, voted, that a Committee be appointed to consider what measures it will be proper for this Society to adopt on the arrival of this our distinguished brother; whose meritorious and disinterested services to our country, in the war of the revolution, cannot be too highly appreciated, and whose whole life has been devoted to the vindication of the rights of man." A committee was then appointed for the purpose, of which Hon. John Brooks (late Governor) was the chairman.

Letters were written to General Lafayette, before he left France by several distinguished individuals, and by the Mayor of New-York and of Boston, in the name and behalf of those corporations, expressing a strong desire, that he would visit America, as it was reported he intended, and informing him of the universal and sincere disposition of the citizens, to present him a tribute of esteem and gratitude.

In a letter dated at Paris, May 26, in reply to the invitation of the citizens of Boston, communicated to him by the Mayor, in their name, under date of March 20th, 1824, he observed, "that amidst the new and high marks of benevolence which the people of the United States and their Representatives had lately deigned to confer upon him, he was proud and happy to recognize those particular sentiments of the citizens of Boston, which had blessed and delighted the first years of his public career, the grateful sense of which had ever been to him a most valued reward and support." "I joyfully anticipate the day," he added, "not very remote, thank God, when I may revisit the cradle of American, and in future, I hope, of *universal* liberty. Your so honorable and gratifying invitation would have been directly complied with, in the case to which you are pleased to allude. [Footnote: This was the particular request that he would land at Boston, if he did not come in a public ship, and feel obliged to arrive at Washington.] But while I profoundly feel the honor intended by the offer of a national ship, I hope I shall incur no blame, by the determination I have taken, to embark as soon as it is in my power, on board a private vessel. Whatever port I first attain, I shall with the same eagerness hasten to Boston, and present its beloved and revered inhabitants, as I have now the honor to offer it to the City Council and to yourself, the homage of my affectionate gratitude and devoted respect."

When this letter of Lafayette was communicated to the Common Council of the city, a large and respectable committee was chosen "to make suitable arrangements for his reception, should he first arrive at the port of Boston; and that on his visiting this city, should he disembark at some other place in the United States, the committee provide for his accommodation, during his residence here; and to adopt all such measures as they might deem proper, to extend to him the hospitality of the city, and to exhibit the feelings of gratitude, which the whole body of citizens entertain for the splendid services, ardent patriotism and private worth of the illustrious visitor."

Hon. Mr. Lloyd, Senator from this State in the Congress of the United States, and particularly attached to Lafayette from family alliances, on hearing of his intended visit to America, also addressed a friendly note to him, at an early day, requesting the honor of receiving him at his hospitable mansion. But the city authorities were desirous, that General Lafayette, who might be justly considered the guest of the people and of the nation, should be accommodated by the city in a more public manner: and Mr. Lloyd, with his usual courtesy and regard to public opinion, resigned his particular claims, although he was among the first and most eminent of the citizens of Boston, to show peculiar and distinguished attention to the favorite of the American people.

In his answer to the letter of Mr. Lloyd, he says, "in whatever part of the United States I shall find myself, on reaching the beloved shore of America, I shall lose no, time in my eagerness to revisit the city of Boston, and answer the flattering invitation I have received. You do justice to the delight I shall feel, at the sight of the felicity and prosperity, which is the reward of a virtuous revolution, founded on the principles of true liberty and self-government."

* * * * *

VISIT OF GENERAL LAFAYETTE

TO THE

UNITED STATES—IN 1824

His arrival was anticipated with great interest and impatience. Preparations were in contemplation, particularly in New-York and Boston, several weeks before he arrived, to receive him with such public marks of veneration and joy, as were justly due to one so distinguished by an ardent love of liberty, and by meritorious exertions for the welfare of our country.

General Lafayette arrived in the harbour of New-York on the morning of the 15th of August, accompanied by his son, George W. Lafayette, and his friend, M. Le Vasseur. A steam boat was in waiting, at the entrance of the harbour, and they were immediately conducted to Staten Island, the residence of the Hon. Mr. Tompkins, Vice President of the United States, where he passed the remainder of the day, being Sunday. This is but a short distance from the city of New-York: here many public characters and other distinguished citizens repaired; on the day of his arrival, to offer him their respectful salutations. The next day he entered this populous city; and his reception was most splendid and cordial. Perhaps no hero of ancient or modern times, if we except the respectful and universal attention paid to Washington, when he made the tour of the United States in 1789, was ever greeted with such a sincere and enthusiastic welcome.

"At an early hour, the whole city was in motion; almost every man, woman and child was preparing to witness the landing of their much respected guest. The shops and stores were closed, and all business was suspended for the day. The ringing of bells, the roar of cannon, and the display of the national flag, at all public places and on board the shipping, proclaimed that it was a day of joy, in which all were anxious to partake. Before 12 o'clock, the battery, the adjoining wharves and every place commanding a view of the passage from Staten Island, were crowded to excess. It was supposed there were nearly 50,000 persons upon the battery, including the troops. This elegant promenade, since its enlargement, is said to be capable of holding nearly the whole population of the city, (130,000) but a large portion of the front was occupied by the brigade of artillery and other troops. The castle garden, almost contiguous to the battery, and its gallery, were also crowded by the citizens.

"Between 10 and 11 o'clock, a large steam ship, manned with about 200 United States seamen, and decorated with the flags of every nation, sailed for Staten Island. She was followed by six large steam boats, all crowded with passengers, decorated with flags, and enlivened by bands of music. In one of them, which exhibited only flags of the United States and of the State of New-York, proceeded the committee of, arrangements of the city, the officers of the United States army and navy, the general officers of the militia, the committee of the Society of Cincinnati, &c. On board this steam boat, General Lafayette embarked at Staten Island, for the city, at about one o'clock. This was announced by a salute from the largest steam ship, manned by the national troops, and from fort Lafayette. The procession then moved for the city, and presented to its inhabitants, a most beautiful and magnificent scene. About two o'clock the General landed at the battery, where he was received by a salute from the troops, and the hearty and reiterated cheers of the immense throng which had assembled to welcome him to our shores.

"It is impossible fully to describe the enthusiasm of joy which pervaded and was expressed by the whole multitude. Here the General had a fair specimen of the affection and respect, which is felt for him by every individual of this extended country. He seemed much moved by these expressions of attachment, and bowed continually to the people who pressed about him. After resting a few moments at the castle garden, he proceeded in an elegant barouche drawn by four horses, escorted by the dragoons and troops, through Broadway to the City Hall. The windows, balconies, and even the roofs of the houses were filled with ladies, all welcoming the General as he passed, by their smiles and waving of handkerchiefs.

"At about 4 o'clock, the procession arrived at the City Hall, where General Lafayette was received by the Mayor and Common Council, and formally welcomed and congratulated on his safe arrival in the country. After receiving the marching salute of the troops in front of the City Hall, he was conducted to the City Hotel, where he dined with the members of the corporation. In the evening, the front of the City Hotel, and many other adjoining buildings, were handsomely illuminated. The theatres and public gardens displayed transparencies; fire-works and rockets in honor of the occasion."— The committee of the Cincinnati waited on General Lafayette, at Staten Island; and were received by him with peculiar marks of affection and friendship. The committee consisted of several field officers of the revolutionary army, some of whom were upwards of eighty years of age.

The following is the address of the Mayor of New-York, to General Lafayette, when he arrived at the city Hall:

"In the name of the municipal authority of the city, I bid you a sincere welcome to the shores of a country, of whose freedom and happiness you will ever be considered one of the most honored and beloved founders. Your contemporaries in arms, of whom indeed but few remain, have not forgot, and their posterity will never forget the young and gallant *Frenchman*, who consecrated his youth, his talents, his fortune and his exertions to their cause; who exposed his life, who shed his blood, that they might be free and happy. They will recollect with profound emotions, so long as they remain worthy of the liberties they enjoy, and of the exertions you made to obtain them, that you came to them in the darkest period of their struggle; that you linked your fortune with theirs, when it seemed almost hopeless; that you shared in the dangers, privations and sufferings of that bitter struggle; nor quitted them for a moment till it was consummated on the glorious field of Yorktown. Half a century has elapsed since that great event, and in that time your name has become as dear to the friends, as it is inseparably connected with the cause of freedom, both in the old and in the new world.

"The people of the United States look up to you as to one of their most honored parents—the country cherishes you as one of the most beloved of her sons. I hope and trust, Sir, that not only the present, but the future conduct of my countrymen, to the latest period of time, will, among other slanders, refute the unjust imputation, that republics are always ungrateful to their benefactors.

"In behalf of my fellow citizens of New-York, and speaking the warm and universal sentiments of the whole people of the United States, I repeat their welcome to our common country."

To this address, General Lafayette replied as follows:—

"SIR,

"While I am so affectionately received by the citizens of New-York and their worthy representatives, I feel myself overwhelmed with inexpressible emotions. The sight of the American shore, after so long an absence; the recollection of the many respected friends and dear companions, no more to be found on this land; the pleasure to recognize those who survive; the immense concourse of a free republican population, who so kindly welcome me; the admirable appearance of the troops; the presence of a corps of the national navy; have excited sentiments, to which no language is adequate: You have been pleased, Sir, to allude to the happiest times, the unalloyed enjoyment of my public life. It is the pride of my heart to have been one of the earliest adopted sons of America. I am proud, also, to add, that upwards of forty years ago I was honored with the freedom of this city. I beg you, Sir; I beg you; gentlemen, to accept yourselves, and to transmit to the citizens of New-York, the homage of my profound and everlasting gratitude, devotion and respect."

On the two following days after his arrival in New-York, General Lafayette received the gratulations of a great number of the citizens;

and on the latter, was addressed by committees of the society of Cincinnati, and of the Historical Society; and also visited the navy yard of the United States. On board of the ship Washington, of 74 guns, his reception was very splendid, and a sumptuous repast was provided. On Thursday, deputations from the Frenchmen resident in the city, and from the gentlemen of the Bar, waited on him, and presented congratulatory addresses.

In his answer to the committee of the Historical Society, he observed,—"The United States are the first nation on the records of history, who have founded their constitution upon an honest investigation and clear definition of their natural and social rights. Nor can we doubt, but that, notwithstanding the combinations made elsewhere by despotism against the sacred rights of mankind, immense majorities in other countries will not in vain observe the happiness and prosperity of a free, virtuous and enlightened people."

To the gentlemen of the Bar, he replied—"Testimonies of esteem from so respectable a body as the Bar of New-York, are highly flattering. I most deeply sympathize, gentlemen, in your regret for the friend (Hamilton) whose prodigious talents made him as eminent in your profession, as he had been is our military, when he deserved Washington's most intimate confidence. The truly republican form of the American constitutions, cannot but endear them to every citizen of the United States. Yet, to any one, who with an American heart, has had opportunities of a comparison with other countries, the blessings of these institutions must appear still more conspicuous."

The address of the French gentlemen in New-York, was very affectionate and respectful, referring, in highly complimentary style, to the services of Lafayette both in France and America. His reply is indicative, at once, of patriotism, of attachment to the cause of rational freedom, and of his regard for the United States, the land of his adoption. "It is a great happiness for me, on my arrival in this land of liberty, to receive the congratulations of my countrymen. At the moment of my departure, the testimonials of affectionate attachment of many of my fellow citizens, the parting accents from the shores of France, left in my heart the most grateful emotions. I delight to participate with you the feelings which I experienced in this happy American land, to which I am bound by so many ties. We also, patriots of 1789, sought to establish the national dignity, the security of property and the happiness of our beautiful France, upon the sacred foundations of liberty and equality. Notwithstanding our misfortunes, the cotemporaries of that epoch will inform you, that the revolution of 1789, has greatly ameliorated the condition of an immense majority of the people. Do not let us despair of the cause of liberty: It is still dear to the hearts of Frenchmen; and we shall one day have the felicity of seeing it established in our beloved country."

During the four days he remained in New-York, all gentlemen and ladies of the most respectable families were individually introduced to him; and he manifested great pleasure at the cordial welcome, with which he was universally greeted. Splendid evening parties were given in honor of the "nation's guest," at which he met many individuals whom he had known more than forty years before. His interviews with "the war-worn veterans," with whom he had been associated in times of danger, for the liberties of the country, were peculiarly interesting and affecting. He embraced them; but his feelings were so powerful, that he could not give utterance to his sentiments for many minutes.

After his arrival at New-York, he early announced his intention to visit Boston, where he had been particularly invited by distinguished individuals, and by the city authorities; especially as the commencement at the University in Cambridge, the literary jubilee of the State, was to be celebrated in a few days. While in New-York, he received invitations by committees or letters from Philadelphia, Albany, New Haven and some other cities, to make a visit to those places respectively; but his desire was first to visit Boston, if possible. Accordingly, he left New-York, where his reception had been so very gratifying to his feelings, and where the citizens were still eager to show him honorable civilities, on Friday morning, for Boston, through New Haven, New London and Providence. He was attended by a committee of the Common Council, the Major General of militia and his suite, the General and field officers of the artillery and infantry, and by strangers and citizens of distinction on horseback, and escorted by the Huzzars of the 2d and 14th regiments, to

Harlem, where he was saluted by the 3d regiment of infantry. On leaving this place, he was saluted by the Lafayette guards of the 2d regiment. The principal part of the troops then returned; and the first regiment of horse artillery continued the escort to the line of Connecticut. A salute was fired at a place called Putnam's hill, on account of the memorable feat performed there by General Israel Putnam, in the revolutionary war. The suite of Lafayette consisted of his son and M. Le Vasseur, who accompanied him in his voyage from France, and four of the Aldermen of New-York. The city corporation had provided an elegant carriage to accommodate him in his journey to Boston, and deputed four of their number to attend him in his route. He traveled with great rapidity, passing the distance of thirty miles in three hours. He appeared perfectly capable of enduring fatigue, and discovered the activity and sprightliness of vigorous manhood.

They reached New Haven about midnight, on his approach to which he was met by the governor's guard, and escorted into that city. Most of the buildings on the principal streets were illuminated, and a national salute was fired. "The night was almost turned into day, and the scene was very brilliant and impressive." He was detained at all the villages on the road from New-York to New Haven, through the eagerness of the citizens, to see and be introduced to this distinguished hero of the revolution. The public road was thronged with multitudes of both sexes and youth, who greeted him with reiterated acclamations; and continued "welcome, welcome." They prepared sincere, though simple offerings of respect to the man, "who fought not for honor or for pay;" but in imitation of his political, American parent, was devoted, life and property, to the cause of our country's freedom. After a public breakfast, a visit to the college, and calls upon Mrs. Trumbull, the widow of the late governor of the state, Hon. Mr. Daggett, senator in Congress, and some other eminent characters, he left New Haven, for New London, Saturday morning, attended by the city authorities and escorted by a company of cavalry, a part of the distance, until met by another troop of horse, by which General Lafayette and suite were then attended to Saybrook, on Connecticut river, about forty miles from New Haven. Part of the Sabbath was passed in New London; and at this place, he attended public worship. He expressed a desire to avoid traveling on that day, as much as possible. At New London, and at most other places on his journey, he met some of his old revolutionary companions, who were delighted to see again in their own free and happy country, a man who had devoted his earliest days and zealous efforts to secure its independence.

He reached Providence on Monday, the 23d, at 12 o'clock, having been met at an early hour, on the boundary line between Connecticut and Rhode Island, by the aids of the Governor of the last named state. When he arrived at the limits of the town of Providence, an immense crowd of citizens were assembled to bid him welcome, and to offer him their hearty gratulations. The houses and streets in the western part of the town, where he entered, were filled with citizens, who greeted him as he passed with reiterated cheers. "When he arrived in front of the State House, he alighted, and was received in a very interesting manner. The avenue leading to the building was lined with female youth, dressed in white, holding in their hands branches of flowers, which they strewed in his path, at the same time waving their white handkerchiefs. Lafayette appeared much gratified and affected by this simple, but touching arrangement. In the senate chamber, he was introduced to the Governor and many other distinguished characters; among whom were several late officers of the revolutionary army. These he embraced with much affection; and his emotions were so great, he was unable to address them. He recognized Captain Olney, the moment he saw him, among a crowd of citizens. This gentleman commanded a company under General Lafayette, at the siege of Yorktown, and was the first to force the redoubts thrown up by the British troops, and carried by our light infantry, in a most brilliant manner, when led on to the assault by their commander in person. At this interview, so affecting and interesting, a thrill ran through the whole assembly, and not a dry eye was to be found among the throng of spectators; while the shouts of the multitude, at first suppressed, and then uttered in a manner tempered by the scene, evinced the deep fueling and proud associations it had excited." Another respectable veteran, of eighty-five years of age, was found among the multitudes assembled to render their affectionate homage to Lafayette. He was a volunteer in the expedition on Rhode Island, in the autumn of 1778, and assisted in conducting the retreat from that place; under direction of the Marquis, when the militia were in great danger from the superior number of the British forces. The aged patriot was overwhelmed with joy, on beholding once more, his beloved general.

On account of a previous engagement to be in Boston, Monday night, or early on Tuesday morning, General Lafayette was obliged, though reluctantly, to leave Providence the afternoon of the day he arrived there. As he left the town he walked some distance, in order to view the troops, which were drawn up in the public street leading towards Boston; and then entered his carriage, accompanied by the Governor and several other public characters; and amidst the cheers of the people proceeded on his journey. He was also attended by the society of Cincinnati of the State of Rhode Island, as far as Pawtucket river, the southern bounds of Massachusetts. When some one expressed an apprehension, that he might be *fatigued* by his rapid traveling and the various scenes through which he passed in the course of the day, he quickly replied, that he experienced too great pleasure, to be sensible of any fatigue.

At Pawtucket, he was met by the aids of Governor Eustis, the Chief Magistrate of the State of Massachusetts, who had been dispatched, the day before, to receive him at the line of the Commonwealth, and to escort him on his way to the capital. Although it was now evening, at several places on the road, large bodies of the militia were collected to salute him; and assemblies of ladies and gentlemen were occasionally met, who offered this illustrious stranger, but respected friend of their country, their tribute of applause and affection. He was too sensible of their sincerity and warmth of their felicitations, not to delay his journey at several villages, and to reciprocate their kind and cordial salutations. It was nearly midnight when he reached the town of Dedham, about ten miles from Boston. Most of the houses in this pleasant village were handsomely illuminated; and a great number of the inhabitants of both sexes were assembled to greet him. During the short pause he was able to make here, he was introduced to many of the principal citizens of the town and vicinity, who had been anticipating his arrival for some hours. When he passed through Roxbury, at about 1 o'clock, he was accompanied by a large cavalcade of citizens of that place and from Boston; and a salute was fired by the Roxbury corps of artillery. His arrival here was also announced by the ascent of rockets from an eminence in the centre of the town; and the note of preparation was thus given for the parade and pleasure of the succeeding day, which had been anticipated with uncommon interest and delight. Lafayette and suite proceeded to the mansion of his Excellency the Governor, to which they had been invited; and the meeting between them was truly affectionate and cordial.

On Tuesday the 24th the inhabitants of Boston hailed the morning light with peculiar emotions, and were abroad at an early hour, preparing for the general testimonies of gratitude and respect to be presented to the "nation's guest." Many of the older citizens recollected him in his youthful days; when he visited the town, *forty-six* years ago, at the request of Congress and Washington, to prevail on the French admiral to co-operate with his fleet in some contemplated attack upon the British Forces. They had not forgotten his zeal and ardor in the cause of America. They knew his great attachment to and respect for the *immortal* chief of the American army, and the confidence, which Washington cherished for Lafayette. Here too were many revolutionary officers and soldiers, who had often witnessed his unwearied activity and personal courage in seasons of difficulty and danger. The Society of Cincinnati in this State contained many of his personal friends, who shared with him in the toils and honors of the war of independence; they had assembled, also, to offer the hand of friendship and affection to their distinguished brother in arms; and to tell him of the happiness which he had been instrumental, with others, in securing to *ten millions* of freemen. The curiosity of the young was awakened to hear of the generous deeds and meritorious services of this celebrated visitor from the old world. They were eager to learn his worth and, his virtues. For they knew their grave and sober sires would not be so greatly moved by the approach of any ordinary character, whatever might be his title or his fame. The sensibility of the female breast was excited to a lively glow, in reflecting upon the character of this eminent foreigner, who had not only given proofs of great devotion to the cause of America, and to the interests of civil liberty, but whose moral and social virtues claimed for him the respect and admiration of all those who loved innocence or commiserated distress. And all classes, without intending to lessen the pre-eminent services and virtues of Washington, who, under providence was the great and chief agent in achieving our independence, and in preserving it, after it had been once established — or to undervalue the important efforts and courage of many other revered heroes and patriots, too numerous to be here named. All, all, were eager to join in the spontaneous offering of gratitude and affection to one so justly celebrated and so *greatly beloved.*

He entered the city, the capital of the state, about 11 o'clock; "and his reception was a triumph and a jubilee. The day was as bright as his laurels, and as mild as his virtues. The various bodies designated to compose the procession, and perform the honors of the day, assembled at an early hour, and at the time appointed." The cavalcade was formed in Common street, at 9 o'clock. It was very numerous, and consisted of the citizens of Boston, of all ranks and classes, on horseback. Proceeding to the extreme southerly part of the city, near the line of Roxbury, they were joined by the Mayor and Aldermen, and members of the Common Council, the Society of Cincinnati, a great number of public civil characters and strangers of distinction, all in carriages; by the general and field officers of the first division of militia, and officers of the army and navy of the United States. An innumerable concourse of people on foot lined the side walks of the spacious street, where the procession was to be formed, the entrance to the city from Roxbury, and fortunately named WASHINGTON-STREET. The cavalcade then proceeded to the mansion of Governor Eustis, which is a short distance, within the town of Rosbury, and escorted General Lafayette and suite to the line, where the city authorities and others, who were to compose the procession, were in waiting to receive him. Here he was greeted by the immense assemblage of citizens, with repeated and enthusiastic acclamations, for several minutes, when the mayor welcomed him with much feeling, in the following speech.

"SIR — The Citizens of Boston welcome you on your return to the United States; mindful of your early zeal in the cause of American Independence, grateful for your distinguished share in the perils and glories of its achievement. — When urged by a generous sympathy, you first landed on these shores, you found a people engaged in an arduous and eventful struggle for liberty with apparently inadequate means, and amidst dubious omens. After a lapse of nearly half a century, you find the same people prosperous beyond all hope and all precedent; their liberty secure; sitting in its strength; without fear and without reproach.

"In your youth you joined the standard of three millions of people, raised in an unequal and uncertain conflict. In your advanced age you return and are met by ten millions of people, their descendants, whose hearts throng hither to greet your approach and rejoice in it.

"This is not the movement of a turbulent populace, excited by the fresh laurels of some recent conqueror. It is a grave, moral, intellectual impulse.

"A whole people in the enjoyment of freedom as perfect as the condition of our nature permits, recur with gratitude, increasing with the daily increasing sense of their blessings, to the memory of those, who, by their labors, and in their blood, laid the foundation of our liberties.

"Your name, sir,—the name of LAFAYETTE, is associated with the most perilous, and most glorious periods of our Revolution;— with the imperishable names of Washington, and of that numerous host of heroes which adorn the proudest archives of American history, and are engraved in indelible traces on the hearts of the whole American people.

"Accept, then, sir, in the sincere spirit in which it is offered, this simple tribute to your virtues.

"Again, sir, the citizens of Boston bid you welcome to the cradle of American Independence, and to scenes consecrated with the blood shed by the earliest martyrs in its cause."

General Lafayette then rose in his carriage, and in a most interesting and felicitous manner, replied as follows:—

"The emotions of love and gratitude, which I have been accustomed to feel on my entering this city, have ever mingled with a sense of religious reverence for the cradle of *American*, and let me hope it will hereafter be said, of *Universal* Liberty.

"What must be, sir, my feelings, at the blessed moment, when, after so, long an absence, I find myself again surrounded by the good citizens of Boston—where I am so affectionately, so honorably welcomed, not only by old friends, but by several successive generations; where I can witness the prosperity, the immense improvements, that have been the just reward of a noble struggle, virtuous morals and truly republican institutions.

"I beg of you, Mr. Mayor, Gentlemen of the City Council, and all of you, beloved citizens of Boston, to accept the respectful and warm thanks of a heart, which has, for nearly half a century, been particularly devoted to your illustrious city."

The reply of the General was received with new plaudits of the assembled people; and "welcome, welcome Lafayette! friend of Washington! friend of America! Friend of liberty!" was repeated again and again; and the heights of Dorchester and Roxbury echoed with the joyful acclamation.

The procession was then formed, and passed through Washington, Milk, Broad, State, Court and Common-streets; to Boylston-street, adjoining the south part of the Common, in the following order—"Three marshals, the Boston corps of Light Dragoons, a battalion of Light Infantry, composed of the Fusiliers, Boston Light Infantry, Winslow Blues, Washington Light Infantry, New-England Guards, Rangers, and City Guards; and a full band of music. Then followed the chief marshal, attended by aids; members of the City Council, Committee of Arrangements, the President of the Common Council and senior Alderman, all in carriages. Here was placed another marshal, immediately preceding the elegant barouche, drawn by four beautiful white horses, in which rode the distinguished GUEST of the city and of the nation, accompanied by the mayor, with marshals also on either side. The son and friend of Lafayette, and gentlemen aldermen from New-York, next followed in carriages; and these were succeeded by the society of the Cincinnati, public characters, Judges and Legislators, and distinguished strangers, in carriages also. Immediately after, two marshals; field and staff officers of the militia, mounted on horseback, and followed also by two marshals. The cavalcade of citizens, of all ranks and in great numbers, with marshals attending, closed the voluntary but triumphant procession.

The dwelling houses and stores on the streets through which the procession was conducted, were crowded with inhabitants in every part. The ladies thus situated, caught the enthusiasm of the occasion, waved their white handkerchiefs, and, with smiles and gladness, greeted the veteran hero, who appeared affected and delighted by these demonstrations of a joyful welcome. The moment Lafayette arrived at the line of the city, the bells struck, and rang merry peals, while the procession was passing through the streets.

Excepting the cavalcade, the procession passed through the Common from Boylston to Park street, on the eastern margin, and between too lines of children of both sexes, belonging to the several schools in the city. Their ages were from about eight to twelve, and nearly three thousand in number. Their dress was neat and uniform; the misses in white, and the masters in white pantaloons and blue spencers. They also wore ribbons in their breasts, stamped with a miniature likeness of Lafayette. As the carriage, in which the general rode, was passing, one of the misses darted from the line where she was standing, and begged to speak with him. She was handed into the carriage, and by the Mayor presented to Lafayette, who pressed an affectionate kiss on her blooming, yet blushing cheek. She had confidence, however, to address him, and to place a wreath of flowers, which she held, on his head. He made her a short but affectionate reply, and placed the wreath on the seat of the carriage. Attached to the wreath of flowers was a small piece of paper, carefully folded, which contained these lines: said to be composed by the mother of the child.

"An infant hand presents these blushing flowers,
Glowing and pure as childhood's artless hours,
Where roses bloom, and buds of *promise* smile,
Repaying with their charms the culturers toil.

Oh! *take them* FATHER, they were culled *for you*!
(Still bright with warm *affection's* sacred dew —)
O let them *live* in thy benignant smile,
And o'er thy *brow of glory* bloom awhile!

'Twined with the *laurel* Fame on thee bestowed
When thy *young heart* with patriot ardor glow'd;

Self exiled from the charms of *wealth* and *love*,
  And, *home*, and *friends*, thou didst *our champion
    prove*,
  And, by the side of Glorious WASHINGTON,
  Didst make our grateful country *all thine own*!

  Go, fragile offering, speak the ardent joy
  Our bosoms feel, which *Time* can ne'er destroy!"

Arches were thrown across several of the principal streets, through which Lafayette was conducted, covered with evergreens and flowers, and containing appropriate mottos. There were two in Washington-street, the largest, and part of the distance, the widest street in the City.—On one of these was very legibly written—"1776—WASHINGTON and LAFAYETTE. *Welcome Lafayette—A Republic not ungrateful.*" On the other

"WELCOME LAFAYETTE."

  "The Fathers in glory shall sleep,
  Who gather'd with thee to the fight;
  But the sons will eternally keep
  The tablet of gratitude bright.
  We bow not the neck
  And we bend not the knee,
  But our hearts, LAFAYETTE,
  We surrender to thee."

The lines were from the pen of a citizen of Boston, whose poetic talents had often delighted the public, and who had received the highest praise from those capable of appreciating the productions of genius.

When the possession arrived at the steps of the State House, near the head of Park Street, salutes were fired by a battalion of artillery on the eminence on the western part of the Common, and at the Navy Yard at Charlestown. Salutes were also fired by a battalion of artillery, placed on the heights of Dorchester, (now South Boston,) when General Lafayette reached the line of the city, at 11 o'clock. The President of the United States had caused an order to be issued, on the first arrival of Lafayette, at New-York, requiring, that he be received by the military officers of the nation, at all public posts, with the salutes and honors due to one of the highest rank in the army.

The Governor and Executive Council of the Commonwealth, were assembled in the spacious Senate Chamber to receive Lafayette in the name of the Representatives of the people, and in pursuance of their resolve of June preceding, as well as in accordance with their own personal feelings and wishes. His Excellency the Governor, here addressed him with great feeling, [Footnote: Governor Eustis was so affected, that he had to call on one of the aids to read the greater part of the address.] in the following concise and pertinent speech:

"SIR, OUR FRIEND,—

"In the name of the government, and in behalf of the citizens of Massachusetts, I have the honor to greet you with a cordial, an affectionate welcome.

"We thank God, that he has been pleased to preserve you through the scenes of peril and of suffering, which have distinguished your patriotic and eventful life, and that we are indulged with this occasion of renewing to you our grateful acknowledgements for the important services which you have rendered to our common country.

"In the last surviving Major General of the American revolutionary army, we recognize a benefactor and friend, from a distant and gallant nation; who, inspired by a love of liberty, subjected himself in his youth, to the toils and hazards of a military life, in support of our rights. Under our illustrious Washington, you were instrumental in establishing the liberties of our country, while your gallantry in the field, secured to yourself an imperishable renown.

"With the enjoyment of the blessings of independence, we shall never cease to associate the name of Lafayette, and our prayer to heaven will be for his health and prosperity."

To which the General, with much animation, replied: —

"SIR,

"When, in the name of the people and government of this State, your Excellency is pleased so kindly to welcome an American veteran, I am proud to share the honors and enjoyments of such a reception with my revolutionary companions and brother soldiers. Sir, I am delighted with what I see, I am oppressed with what I feel; but I depend upon you, as an old friend, to do justice to my sentiments."

Afterwards, a great number of gentlemen were introduced to Lafayette, in the Senate Chamber; of whom were the Judges and other public officers of the United States, of the State and of the City; members of the society of Cincinnati, with their venerable and distinguished President, Hon. John Brooks, late Governor of the Commonwealth. Lafayette recognized his old military and personal friend, at the first sight, and embraced him with great cordiality and affection. Some other veterans of the revolutionary army, who were present, he also recollected; and discovered strong emotions as they approached him and took his hand. Indeed, he was so eager to meet them, that he very generally first seized them, and clung to them with all the affection of a brother. The scene was inexpressibly affecting. There was not a heart untouched — not a cheek unmoistened by the falling tear. To weep then was not weakness; it was proof of gratitude and of a generous feeling, which is an honor to human nature.

By particular request, and to gratify the wishes of the people collected in front of the State House, General Lafayette appeared in the colonnade of this superb edifice, where he was greeted with loud and continued cheers. He was then conducted by the committee of arrangements, to the residence provided for him at the head of Park Street. A public dinner was given by the city authorities, in honor of their noble guest; and the invitation was extended to Senators and members of Congress, the Governor and Ex-Governor of the Commonwealth, judicial and other public characters.

A committee of the society of Cincinnati Called upon General Lafayette at the residence of the Governor, in Roxbury, and before his entrance into Boston. They were anxious to offer him their congratulations at the earliest moment; and to bid him welcome to the land they had unitedly struggled to defend. And a few days after his arrival, the whole society waited on him, when their President made the following address:—

"SIR,

"The Society of Cincinnati of the State of Massachusetts seize the earliest moment after your arrival in this city, of extending to you the hand of friendship and affection. We offer you our most cordial congratulations on your safe arrival again, after the lapse of forty years, on the shores of our favored country, once the theatre of our united toils, privations, and combats with a powerful foe, but now the peaceful domain of a great, a free, and independent people. We hail you, sir, in unison with the millions of our fellow citizens; most respectfully hail you as a Statesman, as a Philanthropist, and as the early, inflexible, and devoted friend, not only of our beloved country, but of the sacred principles of civil liberty and human rights. But we greet you under more tender and hallowed associations; in the endearing relation of a brother-soldier, who, in the ardor of youth commenced in the field with us your career of glory, in the holy cause of Liberty and American Independence.

"But here recollections crowd upon our minds too powerful for utterance. Words would but mock the deep emotions of our hearts should we attempt to express them, in contemplating the character, attributes, and services of the parental Chief, under whose auspices we trod together the field of honor. To the profound veneration and love for his memory that penetrates your bosom, we refer you as to a transcript of our own. It would be vain to imagine the joy that would swell the great mind of Washington, were he still living to recognize with our nation, the generous disinterestedness, the glowing ardor, the personal sacrifices, and the gallant achievements of his much loved Fayette. But it is equally vain to endeavor on this occasion, to exclude such interesting reflections from the mind, or to deny it the melancholy pleasure of lingering on the solemn reality, that not a single individual of the General Staff of the army of the American Revolution now survives to participate in the joy that your presence in the United States has awakened.

"To us it is peculiarly grateful that you are permitted after a lapse of so long a period, to witness the consummation of the principles of our revolution. You will perceive, sir, that the hopes and predictions of the wise and good men who were your particular associates in the arduous struggle, have been fulfilled and surpassed. You will behold a great people united in their principles of jurisprudence, cemented together by the strong ties of mutual interests and happy under the fostering influence of a free and energetic government.

"You will, therefore, allow us to reiterate our felicitations on your safe arrival among us, and to welcome you once more to the good land which your youthful valor contributed to elevate and distinguish.

"May your future life be as tranquil and happy as your past has been useful, uniform, and glorious."

To which the General returned the following answer:

"Amidst the inexpressible enjoyments which press upon my heart, I could not but feel particularly eager and happy to meet my beloved brothers in arms. Many, many, I call in vain; and at the head of them, our matchless paternal Chief, whose love to an adopted son, I am proud to say, you have long witnessed—But while we mourn together, for those we have lost, while I find a consolation, in the sight of their relations and friends, it is to me a delightful gratification, to recognise my surviving companions of our revolutionary army—that army so brave, so virtuous, so united by mutual confidence and affection. That we have been the faithful soldiers of independence, freedom, and equality, those three essential requisites of national and personal dignity and happiness; that we have lived to see those sacred principles secured to this vast Republic, and cherished elsewhere by all generous minds, shall be the pride of our life, the boast of our children, the comfort of our last moments.—Receive, my dear brother soldiers, the grateful thanks, and constant love of your old companion and friend."

On Wednesday was the anniversary of commencement in Harvard University, at Cambridge. The corporation had requested the president, to send a particular invitation to General Lafayette, to be present on the occasion. He had expressed a wish, soon after his arrival at New-York, to attend that literary anniversary. The corporation heard of his intention with great satisfaction. They were sensible of his love of literature, and of his attachment to this ancient seminary. And they remembered, that the governors of the college appreciated his merits *forty years* before, by conferring upon him the highest honors they could bestow. At a meeting of the corporation on the 21st of August, it was voted—

"That the corporation learn with peculiar satisfaction, the intention of General Lafayette to visit this part of our country, at the period of the approaching commencement, and regard the event as auspicious to that joyous and interesting anniversary; and respectfully request, that he will favor the university with his company on that occasion; and thereby afford to the members of the university, and to those who are candidates for its honors, the opportunity of seeing and honoring the distinguished patriot and soldier, whose willing sacrifices and valuable services were devoted to the cause which has secured to the successive races of American youth, the blessings of education in a land of freedom; and whose virtuous and glorious career holds forth to the rising generation, a bright example of the qualities which ought to adorn those, who aspire to aid in the councils, or maintain the rights and interests of a free people."

General Lafayette was escorted from Boson to Cambridge, on Wednesday morning, by a company of cavalry, and accompanied by the Governor and Supreme Executive Council of the Commonwealth. In passing through Cambridge Port, he was gratefully cheered by the assembled citizens, and eloquently addressed by one of the most distinguished, in the name of the whole. The reply of

Lafayette was characteristic and affectionate. He was met by the Corporation and Professors, on his arriving within the precincts of the college, and thus addressed by the learned President Kirkland—

"We bid you welcome, General Lafayette, to the most ancient of the seminaries of our land. The Overseers and Fellows of the University, the Professors and other officers, the candidates for the academic honors of this day, and the students, tender you their respectful, their affectionate salutations. We greet you with peculiar pleasure, at this literary festival, gratified that, you regard the occasion with interest, and espouse the attachment, which as members of a republic, we cannot fail to cherish to the cause of learning and education.

"As a man, sustaining his part through various scenes, prosperous and adverse, of an eventful life, your character and course, marked by moral dignity, have challenged particular respect and sympathy. As the patron, the champion and benefactor of America, you have a relation to us, by which we call you our own, and join gratitude and affection to exalted esteem. The early and costly pledges you gave of devotion to the principles and spirit of our institutions, your adoption of our perilous and uncertain contest for national existence, your friendship in the hour of our greatest need, have associated your name in the minds and hearts of Americans, with the dearest and most affecting recollections. The fathers teach their children, and the instructors their pupils, to hold you in love and honor; and the history of these states takes charge of your claims to the grateful remembrance of all future generations.

"It is a pleasing reflection attending the progress of these communities, that it justifies our friends and supporters; and that the predilections and hopes in our favor, which you indulged in the ardor of youth, have been followed by good auspices till your advanced age. We are, indeed, happy in presenting you the fruit of your toils and dangers, in the kindly operation of the causes, which you did so much to call into action, and we rejoice in every demonstration we are able to give, that your care for us has not been vain. Knowing how you feel yourself to have a property in our welfare, and sensible of the enjoyment accruing to your generous spirit from our prosperity, we find in these considerations, new motives to maintain liberty with ardor; and in the exercise of our functions, feel bound to endeavour to send out from our care, enlightened and virtuous men, employing their influence to secure to their country the advantages, and prevent and remedy the evils attending the wide diffusion among a people of political power.

"Accept our wishes and prayers for your health and happiness. May the Invisible Hand which has been your safeguard thus far, continue its protecting care. May the Supreme Disposer, the Witness and Judge of character and conduct, having appointed you a long and tranquil evening of days, receive you to the final and glorious reward of the faithful in a perfect state."

The following is the substance of the General's reply: —

"It is with real pleasure, sir, that I find myself again at this University, which I visited for the first time, more than forty years ago. The great improvements which have been made here during the interval, are striking evidences of the tendency of liberal political institutions, to promote the progress of civilization and learning. I beg, you to accept my warmest thanks for your kind expressions of personal civility to myself, and my best wishes for the continued prosperity of the valuable establishment over which you preside."

When he entered the place provided for the celebration of commencement, where a numerous company of ladies and gentlemen had assembled, to attend the ceremonies and literary performances of the day, there was an instantaneous and universal acclamation; not stunning and boisterous; but the decorous and chastened greeting of an intelligent audience. When he, reached the stage, he bowed repeatedly to the assembly, with great apparent sensibility. Several of the young gentlemen, alluded to him in their orations; and some dwelt particularly on his early devotion to the cause of America in the struggle for independence, with great effect. These notices, though short and indirect, were calculated to excite the grateful recollections of the audience; who responded to the sentiments with enthusiastic acclamations.

Thursday and Saturday mornings, for several hours, he received the personal compliments and congratulations of a great number of the inhabitants of Boston and vicinity, of both sexes. They were presented to him, on the spacious area of the ground floor of the

State House. The house provided for his residence while in the city, though unusually large, was not well adapted for such crowds of visitors as pressed to behold him. Many aged people were presented, who had served with him in the revolutionary war, or recollected events of that period, which they were desirous to relate. Some were on crutches, and others bared their arms to show the honorable scars occasioned by the bayonet or ball of the enemy, in the "glorious fight" for freedom. Some could boast of having fought under his command, or by his side, at Brandywine and Monmouth; and others, that followed in his path of peril and glory in Virginia, in 1781, and assisted in successfully storming the redoubt at Yorktown, on the memorable evening of the 15th of October, which decided the fate of Cornwallis.

He seized the hands of these his old companions in arms, with great eagerness and emotion; and while they, in the honest pride of their souls related their "hair-breadth escapes," which led the spectators almost to envy their claims to such honourable boasting, the veteran hero exclaimed, "O my brave Light Infantry! My gallant troops!"—Several aged citizens who were personally engaged in opposing the British forces who marched to Lexington and Concord, for the purpose of destroying the Provincial stores collected at the latter place, were present at this interview. A gun was also shown to General Lafayette, from which was fired the ball, which killed the first of the regular troops slain on that memorable occasion. These meetings revived recollections important to be preserved, and served to remind the rising generations of the principles and deeds of their fathers. We trust they did not awaken any angry or hostile feelings towards an ancient enemy; but served only to kindle our gratitude to Almighty God, for his gracious interpositions in our behalf, and to perpetuate our respect for the remains of those who offered up their lives for our freedom and welfare.

On Thursday, by particular request of the literary society of "*Phi Beta Kappa*," so called, in the university, General Lafayette attended the celebration of their anniversary at Cambridge. It was never known before, that any one, however distinguished either for literature or virtue, was invited to dine with the society, unless a member of some other branch of the association. The departure in this case, from the invariable usages and rules of the society, is proof of the very high estimation in which Lafayette is held, and of the disposition, in all classes of citizens, to manifest their respect for his character. He proceeded to the university, about 1 o'clock, when he was again greeted with the hearty cheers of the citizens, as he passed the high-way, and when he arrived. The public performances on this occasion, were an oration and a poem. The latter was prepared at very short notice, and had particular reference to the visit of the illustrious hero and philanthropist, Lafayette. It purported to be the vision of the *Genius of Liberty*. It was a felicitous effort of the poetic muse. The gradual but certain dissolution of ancient despotic systems was predicted, as by the spirit of inspiration; and the blessings and joys of well regulated freedom were described with a masterly pencil, as extending and spreading in all parts of the civilized world. It was the electrifying voice of genius speaking to hearts full of gratitude and swelling with joyous emotions.

The orator was not less happy in his subject, nor less ingenious and eloquent in its illustration. His object was to present, in all its force, the motive to intellectual and literary effort. He assumed the progressive nature of the human mind; referred to the advances already made in science and the arts, and in civil governments; noticed the tendencies in society to higher improvements; and glanced at the facilities for social happiness and intellectual and moral excellence, in this western world, under our mild and republican institutions. It was an uncommon display of talent and research, and of profound observations on the present, improved and improving condition of man. He pointed out the happy destiny which awaited the United States, which a powerful imagination had predicted, but which sober facts also authorize us to expect; and called upon the literary and patriotic youth of our country to use all honorable efforts for hastening on this glorious issue. In speaking of the wisdom, firmness and courage of our patriotic fathers, by whom our liberties were secured, and our independence established, he paid a just tribute to the disinterested and heroic services of Lafayette, who cherished and aided our cause in the most gloomy periods of the war. The reference was most appropriate; and the statement of his zeal and efforts in our behalf, produced such a deep conviction of his devotion to America, and of his influence in obtaining the support of France, which, probably, saved our country from subjugation, that a deep and strong emotion was produced in the whole immense concourse; which, subdued as it was for a time, burst forth, at last, in overwhelming and almost convulsive agitations. The orator seemed not to aim at such an extraordinary impression. He reminded his hearers indeed of "truths surpassing fiction;" he brought to their recollection past scenes of danger endured, the generous and heroic deeds performed — he spake of the "Paternal Chief," who was the guide and support of other brave spirits, now laid low in the silence of death — The effect was wonderful: the whole audience were melted into tears of mingled gratitude and respect; gratitude for such patriotic services, and of respect for the memories of men, who had secured the blessings of civil liberty to the immense and increasing population of this extensive country. Lafayette was very sensibly affected, by this unexpected expression of gratitude for his early services, and by the strong emotions manifested by the assembly, at the name of Washington. The hours passed in the dining hall were consecrated to reminiscences of the interesting events which occurred in the revolutionary contest, to grateful recollections of the statesmen and heroes, who advocated and defended the cause of freedom, and thus led the way in the glorious march of human improvement and happiness, which the present generation is so rapidly pursuing. Here were assembled the judges of the land, the ministers of religion, the legislators of the state and nation, several of the heroes of the revolution, and numerous eminent literary characters from various parts of the United States, to unite with the younger sons of Harvard, in offerings of affectionate gratitude to a man, who had no gifts of power or titles of honor to bestow; but whose useful services and uniform course of honorable and benevolent purpose, in their estimation, claimed a higher tribute than was due to sceptered princes, or the most renowned conquerors of ancient or modern times.

On Friday morning, committees from Portsmouth, Portland, Newport, Haverhill, Newburyport, Plymouth, and from Bowduin College, inviting him to visit those respective places; where the people were desirous to see him, and to offer personally their welcome salutations. He was unable to comply with these flattering invitations, as he had engaged to return to New-York, at an early day. But he received these testimonies of attachment with great sensibility; and expressed a hope to visit them before his final departure from the United States. He left his place of residence in Boston at 10 o'clock, accompanied by Governor Eustis and suit, Governor Brooks, the deputation from New-York, the Mayor and committee of arrangements of Boston, and proceeded to Charlestown, which he previously engaged to visit, at this time. As he passed through the streets in the north part of the city, the people pressed around him, testifying their regard, and cheering him on his way with repeated acclamations. Raised arches, wreathes of evergreen, and variegated colours added to the brilliancy of the scene. He was met at the centre of the bridge, which is the dividing line between Boston and Charlestown, by the Chief Marshal and his aids, and conducted to the square, where a committee of the citizens of that town was in waiting to receive him. A procession was then formed, headed by two marshals, and escorted by a regiment of light infantry, and a battalion of artillery, with martial music, consisting of the committee of arrangements, General Lafayette, his son and friend who accompanied him from France; the Governor and suite, Governor Brooks and General Dearborn, Judges of the Courts and members of the Supreme Executive Council of the State; deputation from New-York, Mayor and committee of Boston, officers of the army and navy of the United States, and of the militia of the State; strangers of distinction, and civil officers of the town of Charlestown. It proceeded to Bunker Hill, where the chairman of the committee of the town, addressed Lafayette as follows: —

"SIR,

"In behalf of the inhabitants of Charlestown, the committee of arrangements present their respectful salutations to General Lafayette, and bid him a cordial welcome to this town. This joyful occasion revives high national feelings and recollections, and touches the springs of gratitude by reminding us of that interesting period of our history, which gave to our country a gallant hero, and to the rights of mankind a steadfast champion. While we participate in the thrill of delight, which every where hails the visit of our illustrious friend, we cannot suppress the peculiar emotion of our hearts on receiving you, sir, on the memorable heights of *Bunker*. On this holy ground, immortalized by the dead, and sacred to the manes of revolutionary heroes: Over these heights, liberty once moved in blood and tears;—her chariot on wheels of fire. Now she comes to her car of peace and glory; drawn by the affections of a happy people, to crown on these same heights, with civic honors, a favorite son, whose early strength was given to her sacred struggles, and whose riper years are now permitted to behold the splendor of her triumphs. In the fullness of our hearts we give thanks to Almighty God, who has guided and guarded your high career of peril and renown.

"Permit us, beloved General, again to welcome you to our borders;—to express our ardent hopes, that your valuable life may be prolonged to the utmost limits of earthly happiness;—that the land which has been enriched with the dew of your youth, may be honored as the asylum of your old age;— that the country which now blends your fame with the mild lustre of Washington, may henceforth hail you as a citizen of Washington's country;— and that, during the residue of your years, you may live amidst the attentions, as you will forever live in the hearts of a grateful and admiring people."

To this address the General replied—

"With profound reverence, sir, I tread this holy ground, where the blood of American patriots—the blood of Warren and his companions, early and gloriously spilled, aroused the energy of three millions, and secured the happiness of ten millions, and of many other millions of men in times to come. That blood has called both American continents to republican independence, and has awakened the nations of Europe to a sense, and in future, I hope, to the practice of their rights. Such have been the effects of a resistance to oppression, which was, by many pretended wise men of the times, called rashness; while it was duty, virtue;—and has been a signal for the emancipation of mankind.

"I beg you, sir, and the magistrates, and the citizens of Charlestown, to accept the homage of my gratitude for your kind welcome, and of those sentiments of affection and respect, which, for so many years, I have cherished toward their town."

While on this memorable eminence, he was informed by Governor Brooks, of the recent association for erecting a monumental pillar on that hallowed spot, to perpetuate the remembrance of the justly celebrated battle of the 17th of June, 1775; when a few regiments of undisciplined militia, made a brave stand against a large regular British force, commanded by generals of great experience and courage. This great event, so important in the annals of our country, as it convinced the English government of the resolution of the colonies to maintain the liberty which they claimed, and of the daring courage of the American people. This event is to be commemorated in June next, when fifty years will be completed, by an oration, and other public appropriate services and ceremonies. General Lafayette expressed great satisfaction of the proposal. He requested that he might be considered a subscriber for the monument; and assured the gentlemen present, that it would be his wish and endeavour to attend the celebration.

General Lafayette availed of this opportunity to visit the navy yard, in Charlestown, belonging to the United States, in compliance with a previous invitation from the officer commanding on the station: and he appeared highly gratified with the establishment in all its departments. He agrees entirely with those enlightened politicians of our own country, who have always considered a naval force of great advantage to America, if not absolutely necessary to our Independence. He dined this day with his Excellency the Governor, in company with several revolutionary veterans, and a large number of public characters of this and the neighbouring states, who were then on a visit to the capital.

Saturday, after receiving the salutations of the citizens, who were desirous of being presented to him, he set off for Medford, to visit his particular and valued friend, Governor Brooks. His reception in this beautiful village, is represented as very interesting. The citizens had comparatively short notice of the visit to that place; but they greeted him with great cordiality, and the honors bestowed were not unworthy of their distinguished guest. The main streets and the houses which he passed before he reached the mansion of Governor Brooks, were filled with children and people, who repeatedly bid him welcome, with great cordiality, and expressed their gratitude and joy on beholding the man, who they had learned, had done so much for their beloved country; and who was the respected friend of one among them, whom they always delighted to honor. A company of artillery fired a salute, as he entered the village; and several arches were thrown across the street, decorated with flags, and wreaths of flowers and evergreens. Under one of them he was met by the selectmen, one of whom thus addressed him —

"GENERAL LAFAYETTE,

"The selectmen of Medford, as the representatives of the town, deem it a grateful and honorable part of their duty to bid you welcome.

"They are proud, sir, that Medford is the birthplace of one of your companions in arms — a man, who by his bravery in the field, his patriotism and civic virtues, contributed to acquire as much glory to our country, as honor to himself.

"We rejoice, sir, that you both live to meet again, and to enjoy together the consolations fairly derived from your virtuous and heroic deeds.

"The minds of our countrymen traced your course with anxious solicitude, through the French revolution, from your first success in the cause of liberty, until the spirit of oppression confined you to a dungeon; and their hearts were gladdened, when, by the influence of our great and good Washington, their friend was at last set free. In the rich harvest you are now gathering of the expressions of esteem and gratitude of this numerous people, whose freedom and happiness your exertions so essentially contributed to establish, we hope you will find some compensation for all your trials, sacrifices and sufferings; and we feel much complacency, that, in this respect you have gained so complete a triumph over the monarchs of the world.

"Again sir, we bid you a most cordial welcome; and hope, the testimonials of approbation you are receiving from every heart and every tongue, will forever retain an instructive lesson to mankind, that patriots who endure. faithfully to the end, shall not lose their reward."

The General said in reply—"I am most happy in visiting my old brother soldier and friend, General Brooks, to be received with so kind a welcome: You speak of *compensation*, sir; the smallest part of the delight which I have experienced in America, would more than repay me for all my services and all my sufferings."

Several evening parties were given in honor of Lafayette, while he was in Boston, by some of its most distinguished citizens. On these occasions, he manifested great pleasure on meeting the children or relatives of the patriots of our revolution, with many of whom he had a personal acquaintance. It was delightful to observe the eagerness with which the ladies, old and young, pressed around him and the pride with which they boasted of hawing taken his hand. His countenance and manner discovered the joy which filled his heart, in cherishing recollections of past services, which he might indulge without vanity; and in perceiving the gratitude, which a deep sense of those services excited among all classes. He manifested a desire to attend the religious service of the Sabbath at the church in Brattle-street, where he had formerly joined in worship with Bowdoin, Hancock and Cooper; he was accordingly conducted there, accompanied by the Mayor of the City and Chief Justice of the State. The sermon, by the learned and pious pastor of that Church, which was an occasional one, was happily calculated to direct and chasten the feelings of the audience. He inculcated the sacred duty of confidence and joy in the providence and moral government of God, and of gratitude to those who had been raised up to be instruments of extensive blessings to our country. The most ardent were gratified, while the more sober and devout were pleased, that no complimentary panegyric was pronounced incompatible with the solemnity of the place and day. In the afternoon he visited. Hon. John Adams at Quincy; the truly venerable patriot of 1775; a decided, zealous advocate for independence in 1776; the able and faithful minister of the nation, at foreign courts; and sometime President of the United States. Mr. Adams is eighty-eight years of age, and his constitution much debilitated within a few years. But his powerful mind is still bright and vigorous; and he dwells with great enthusiasm upon the glorious prospects of our rising empire. His highly valuable services to the country can never be forgotten. For no one, if Washington be excepted, among the many firm asserters of our rights in the struggle for independence, could justly claim a greater portion of gratitude and praise from the present generation.

Desirous of offering all due honors to General Lafayette, and knowing his taste for military exhibitions, the Governor ordered the militia of Boston, which constituted a brigade, of the first division, and an equal number from Essex and Middlesex, which included the second and third divisions, to assemble on the Common in the city of Boston, on Monday, the 30th of August; This was really a proud day, particularly for the citizen soldiers of Massachusetts; but *all* classes of the people enjoyed this imposing and honorable display. For our militia are justly considered the ornament as well as the defence of the republic. Citizens of all professions take an interest in their appearance, their discipline and their reputation. The ranks are composed of our valuable and industrious population; and their officers are to be found among our respectable mechanics, merchants and professional gentlemen. The exhibition was the most splendid of the kind recollected by the oldest inhabitants. There were above five thousand men armed and equipped, and their appearance and movements would have done credit to regular troops. Their officers are men of talents and ambition. The impression made upon the minds of a great concourse of distinguished citizens, in the civil department, who were present, was highly creditable to our military system, and to those, whose duty it is to attend to the execution of laws on the subject. The Governor, as Commander in Chief, had ordered a spacious marque to be erected, where upwards of fifteen hundred people were accommodated in partaking of an abundant collation; rations were also dealt out to all the troops on duty at the expense of the State. The spectacle was most magnificent. The officers and soldiers did themselves and the State great honor by their exact discipline and soldierly appearance; and by the promptness and regularity of their movements. The illustrious visitor was highly pleased, the strangers were gratified; and the militia themselves felt a conscious pride, in having an opportunity to offer appropriate salutations to one who was both a soldier and a philanthropist.

Should it be supposed by the sober citizens of other countries, or by those in our own, who did not join in these offerings of grateful admiration to Lafayette, and who therefore could have felt nothing of the enthusiasm which such scenes are calculated to produce; that there was too much parade or an undue measure of sensibility manifested on this occasion; it may be proper to observe, that no conclusion is to be drawn from this great rejoicing, that the people of Boston, or in fact of the United States, are disposed to pay higher regard to eminent men of the military than in the civil department; or that they have so little discrimination, as to bestow applause upon merely splendid achievements. It is believed to be a fact, that the most intelligent and sober part of the community were as ready to engage in these processions and ceremonies as those of the more common and uninformed class of citizens. How could it be otherwise? These are convincing proofs of the zeal, disinterestedness and devotion of General Lafayette to the cause of American liberty and independence—of his bravery, activity, judgment, constancy and fidelity—of his attachment to Washington and other patriots, and of their regard for him; and of his uniform support of regulated liberty in his own country. In his early days, he had risked every thing and had done every thing which an individual could possibly endure or attempt, in our behalf. He had now in advanced life, left his own beloved retirement in a distant hemisphere, to visit this land of liberty, and of his affections; to behold the prosperity, order, enjoyment and felicity of a great people. His character, too, is unstained by bloodshed and crime; it is consecrated on the contrary by the prayers, and tears and benedictions, of all good men in America and Europe. Who then will censure or wonder, that he should be received by the moral and sober people of America, with all that cordiality and enthusiasm, which were discovered on his arrival among us? We do not forget Washington; our beloved, and almost adored Washington—nor are we insensible to the merits and virtues of other statesmen and heroes of our own country. But, surely we may be allowed to greet this old distinguished benefactor, with a cordial welcome, without subjecting ourselves to the charge of extravagance or caprice.

The character of the militia in Boston, and generally through the state, has been much improved within the last fifteen years. They have recently adopted a cheap uniform; and great improvements have been made in adopting the modern system of tactics. The independent companies need not decline a comparison with regular troops; and, what is very important to the respectability of the militia, their officers are intelligent and ambitious, and actuated by a patriotic spirit, which is a pledge of fidelity and a stimulus to honorable exertion. The high praise bestowed upon the militia at this review, was justly merited.

General Lafayette left Boston on Tuesday morning for Portsmouth, in the state of New Hampshire, intending to pass through Marblehead, Salem and Newburyport, on his way to the former place. A number of distinguished citizens, and a Committee of the City Council accompanied him to the northern line of the city; and the governor's aids attended him to the extreme part of the state adjoining New Hampshire. On his route, he was greeted by the inhabitants of Chesea, Lynn and Marblehead, with great feeling and respect, alike honourable to themselves and gratifying to the friend and guest of the nation. Addresses were also made to him, in these several towns, expressive of their gratitude for his services, and of the lively sense they had of his present visit to the country. He took breakfast at Marblehead, where almost the whole population of this industrious and patriotic town were presented to him. He also met here, some gentlemen celebrated for their naval exploits in the war of the revolution.

His reception at Salem was very distinguished and splendid. At the entrance of the town, he was met by the selectmen and committee, a numerous cavalcade, and a large body of citizens in carriages, and received a salute of artillery; on advancing a short distance within the bounds of the town, the bells commenced ringing, and the escort was joined by a battalion of light infantry, and a body of seamen, of about two hundred, in blue jackets and white trousers, with ribbons on their hats, stamped with the name of Lafayette.

"With the hearty cheers of these hardy sons of Neptune, the General appeared to be peculiarly impressed. Over South Salem bridge were two tastefully decorated arches—one bearing the inscription "WELCOME ILLUSTRIOUS CHIEF! *Receive the pledges of thy Children to sustain with fidelity the principles that first associated* LAFAYETTE *with the destinies of America*." These arches were surrounded by an immense number of citizens, who made the air ring with their huzzas and welcomes. The figure of an Indian Chief characteristically dressed, bore labels inscribed *"Lafayette and Liberty. Welcome generous Lafayette."*

"The procession passed through the principal streets, which were thronged with spectators; while the windows of the houses were crowded with females, all eager to see and welcome the heroic visitor.

"Civic Arches, historical and patriotic Inscriptions, memorable eras, wreaths of flowers and evergreens, banners and flags, were displayed in many of the streets, enlivening the scene, animating the cheers, and affording grateful recollections.

"Central street was gaily dressed in colours, and on an elegant arch were inscribed the names of distinguished patriots of the revolution, crowned with those of WASHINGTON and LAFAYETTE. In North-street a similar arch bore the inscription: — *"Honor to him who fought and bled for the peace and happiness we now enjoy."* On an arch at Buffum's corner, was inscribed, "LAFAYETTE, *the friend of Liberty, we welcome to the land of liberty. He did not forget us in our adversity — In our prosperity we remember his services with gratitude."* Near the above, another arch bore a likeness of Lafayette, surmounted by an eagle.

"Near the avenue leading to the bridge at which, in February, 1775, Col. LESLIE, with a detachment of the British 64th regiment, met with a repulse in an attempt to carry off some canon deposited in the vicinity, were banners, with the following inscription: —

"Leslie's Repulse, 1775. *Lafayette's Renown,* 1824."

"In Winter-street an arch bore the following inscription on American duck, made at the factory in Salem —

AMERICAN DUCK

"While winds shall blow, and seas shall roll,
While aught remains that's good and great,
Our *Native Duck,* from pole to pole,
Shall waft the fame of Lafayette."

"Washington-square was decorated with two arches, tastefully ornamented, one bearing the name of the General in oaken characters and the second a bust of Washington.

"On Washington-square the General passed between two lines of boys, about one thousand in number, arrayed under their respective instructors, all bearing Lafayette badges. One of the gates of the square bore this inscription. — "*The children welcome with joy, the illustrious benefactor of their fathers.*" And as the General passed, they shouted "*Welcome Lafayette.*"

"Notwithstanding the heavy rain, this youthful band could not be prevailed upon to leave the ground, but remained bravely at their post until they had shared with their parents in the honor and happiness of greeting the nation's guest.

"From Washington-square the procession passed to the Coffee-House, now named *Lafayete Coffee-House* (late *Essex;*) where, on a temporary stage, erected in front of the house, the Committee of Arrangements received their illustrious guest, and Judge Story, the president of the day, in the most interesting and eloquent manner, welcomed him in the following address: —

"General LAFAYETTE.

"SIR — Forty years have elapsed since the inhabitants of this town had the pleasure to welcome you within its limits. Many, who then hailed your arrival with pride and exultation, have descended to the grave, and cannot greet you on your long desired, return. But, thanks to a good providence, many are yet alive, who recollect with grateful sensibility, the universal joy of that occasion. Your disinterested zeal in embarking is a cause, deemed almost hopeless — your personal sacrifices in quitting a home, endeared by all the blessings with which affection and virtue can adorn life — your toils and perils in the conflicts of war, and the vicissitudes of a discouraging service — your modest dignity and enthusiasm on receiving the homage of a free people — these were all fresh in their memories, and gave an interest to the scene, which cannot be described, but which time has hallowed with his most touching grace. I stand now in the presence of some, venerable in age and character, who were the delighted witnesses of that interview, and whose hearts again glow with the feelings of that happy day.

"To us of a younger generation—the descendants of your early friends and companions in arms, a different but not less interesting privilege belongs. We are allowed the enviable distinction of meeting in his riper years, one, whom our fathers loved in their youth. We welcome you to our country, to our homes, to our hearts. We have read the history of your achievements, your honors, and your sufferings! They are associated with all that is dear to us—with the battle-grounds, consecrated by the blood of our heroes— with the tender recollections of our departed statesmen—with the affectionate reverence of our surviving patriots. Can we forget that our country was poor and struggling alone in the doubtful contest for Independence, and you crossed the Atlantic at the hazard of fortune, fame and life, to cheer us in our defence? That you recrossed it to solicit naval and military succors from the throne of France, and returned with triumphant success? That your gallantry checked in the southern campaigns, the inroads of a brave and confident enemy? That your military labours closed only with the surrender at Yorktown, and thus indissolubly united your name with the proud events of that glorious day? We cannot forget these things if we would—We would not forget them if we could. They will perish only when America ceases to be a nation.

"But we have yet higher sources of gratification on the present occasion. You have been not merely the friend of America, but of France, and of liberty throughout the world. During a long life in the most trying scenes, you have done no act for which virtue need blush or humanity weep. Your private character has not cast a shade on your public honors. In the palaces of Paris and the dungeons of Olmutz, in the splendor of power, and the gloom of banishment, you have been the friend of justice, and the asserter of the rights of man. Under every misfortune, you have never deserted your principles. What earthly prince can afford consolation like this? The favor of princes, and the applause of senates, sink into absolute nothingness, in comparison with the approving conscience of a life devoted to the good of mankind. At this very moment you are realizing the brightest visions of your youth, in the spectacle of ten millions of people prosperous and happy under a free government, whose moral strength consists in the courage and intelligence of its citizens. — These millions welcome your arrival to the shores of the west with spontaneous unanimity; and the voice which now addresses you, feeble as it is, repeats but the thoughts that are ready to burst from the lips of every American."

The General's reply was in his usual manner. — It was brief, affectionate, and full of feeling.

An impressive circumstance occurred in the delivery of the address. — When the Judge came to that part which says, *"We could not forget them if we would; we would not forget them, if we could;"* the spontaneous assent of the assembled people to the sentiment, was given by *"No, never;"* repeated by thousands of voices, and accompanied by deafening shouts of applause.

A great number of introductions to the General took place. Of them, were several revolutionary officers and soldiers.

At Beverly and Ipswich he received from the assembled inhabitants, the same cordial welcome with which he had been greeted in other towns, through which he passed. The selectmen of these places waited on him, and offered him the congratulations of their fellow citizens; the people greeted him with repeated cheers of *"welcome, welcome Lafayette;"* and arches were erected at several public places, containing appropriate mottoes. The houses of the villages through which he passed, after the evening set in, were brilliantly illuminated.

It was evening when he arrived at Ipswich, and the weather was very inclement. The inhabitants had, therefore, assembled in the meeting house to receive him. Thither he was conducted by a committee of the town; and on his entrance, he was greeted with great exultation and joy. One of the committee addressed him as follows: —

"GENERAL LAFAYETTE,

"Accept from the people of Ipswich, their cordial congratulations on your arrival in their country and within their own borders. To this ancient town, sir, we bid you a joyful welcome.

"Having devoted to our beloved country, in her weak and critical situation, the vigor of your youth and the resources of a mind intent on the cause of freedom and humanity, and committed to a common lot with her, your own destinies,—that country can never forget the services you rendered, and the sacrifices you incurred, for her defence and protection, when assailed by overbearing power.

"We rejoice in having an opportunity of presenting ourselves in this house, consecrated to the worship of the God of our fathers, who has kindly raised up friends and patrons of the cause of our country and of liberty, to pay to you our grateful respect for your eminent labours.

"Most of those who acted in, or witnessed the great scenes in which you bore so conspicuous a part, have now descended to the tombs of their fathers. The present generation can rehearse only what they have heard with their ears, and their fathers have told them. But the name of Lafayette is not confined to any generation. While the liberties of America shall endure, it will descend from father to son, associated with those of the immortal Washington, and other heroes and sages of our revolution, as the friend of our country, of liberty, and of man.

"Illustrious benefactor—may the blessing of Heaven ever attend you, and may your remaining days be as happy, as your past have been perilous, useful and honorable."

To which the General made the following reply:—

"SIR,

"The attentions paid me by my American friends, I receive with inexpressible gratitude. I regret that so many of my friends here, should be exposed on my account to this storm. I have ever considered it my pride and my honor, that I embarked in the cause of Independence in this country; and I rejoiced when I found myself again landed on the American shores. You, kind sir, the people of this town, and all who are assembled in this solemn place, will please to accept my thanks for this expression of your attachment, and receive my best wishes for your individual prosperity and happiness."

He reached Newburyport a little past ten o'clock, where he passed the night. His lodgings were the same which Washington occupied, when he made his tour through the northern states, in 1789, the first year of his presidency. The following address was made to him, by the chairman of a committee of that town: —

"GENERAL LAFAYETTE,

"The citizens of Newburyport are happy in this opportunity of greeting, with the warmest welcome, a distinguished benefactor of their country.

"The important services, which you rendered this people in the day of their distress; the devotedness which you manifested in their perilous cause, and the dangers which you *sought* for their relief, are incorporated in our history, and firmly engraved upon our hearts.

"We would lead you to our institutions of learning, charity and religion; we would point you to our hills and valleys covered with flocks, and smiling in abundance, that you may behold the happy effects of those principles of liberty, which you was so instrumental in establishing.

"Our children cluster about you to receive a patriot's blessing. Our citizens press forward to show their gratitude. Our nation pays you a tribute, which must remove the reproach that republics are ungrateful.

"As the zealous advocate for civil liberty, we bid you welcome; as the brave defender of an oppressed people, we make you welcome; as the friend and associate of our immortal Washington, we bid you welcome."

General Lafayette replied in his usually courteous and animated manner, and evincing his great sensibility to the kind and friendly greetings with which he had been received. He here also met several veterans of the revolutionary army; a gratification which he enjoyed in almost every place he visited. Though the number is rapidly lessening, a few remain in most of the populous towns of the Commonwealth.

He left Newburyport Wednesday morning for the capital of New-Hampshire. The escort contemplated to have attended on his way to the bounds of the state, was prevented by the heavy rain. It was at his urgent request that it was dispensed with. The committee of the town however, accompanied him to Hampton; where he was met by a deputation from Portsmouth, and conducted on his intended route. When passing through Greenland, a procession of the citizens was formed, by which he was attended through the villages. Here he was welcomed also by salutes from an artillery company, by civic arches and repeated acclamations of the assembled people. One of the arches was supported by two young ladies, representing LIBERTY and PEACE. One presented him a wreath, adorned with flowers, and said, "*Venerable sire, condescend to receive this emblem of the hero's glory, as the token of a nation's gratitude and love.*" The other presented him the olive branch, saying, "*Good and faithful servant, peace and happiness await you.*" He received these with complacency, took each young lady by the hand, and made an affectionate reply.

He then proceeded to Portsmouth, where he arrived about noon. He was conducted into this town by an escort on horseback, and a procession of carriages, (the whole extending two miles) composed of the civil, judicial and legislative authorities; officers of the United States and of New-Hampshire, &c. &c. The margins of the avenue leading to the centre of the town, was lined with children, with the inhabitants of both sexes in the rear; who greeted him with their cordial welcomes and repeated acclamations. Salutes were fired, and the bells rang a joyous peal; and the streets through which the procession passed, were crowned with arches, decorated with wreaths of evergreen and garlands of flowers. The procession moved through several streets to Franklin Hall: and here, when General Lafayette alighted, the chairman of the selectmen addressed him thus:—

"SIR,

"The selectmen of Portsmouth, in behalf of their fellow citizens, most respectfully and heartily bid you welcome.

"Enjoying, as we do, the happiness of a free government, we cannot but feel grateful to all, by whose exertions it was obtained. Those intrepid men among ourselves, who in the hour of danger stood forth in defence of their country's rights, have a lasting claim upon our regard. But in contending for the liberty of their country, they were striving to secure their own happiness, and the prosperity of their children. *They* found a motive for exertion in their own interest; which, while it derogates nothing from the value of their services, places in a strong light, the pure zeal and contempt of private advantage, which led *you* to our aid, from the shores of a foreign land. *Their* love of liberty was necessarily the sentiment of patriotism; *yours* was an ardent desire for the general welfare of mankind.

"After an absence of forty years from our country, most of which have been passed in scenes of unexampled excitement and perplexity, it gives us peculiar pleasure to find you still the firm and consistent friend of liberal principles. We have watched the progress of your eventful life, with unaffected sympathy; and whether at the head of the National Guards, in the dungeons of Magdeburg and Olmutz, or in the Chamber of Deputies, we have found nothing to lessen our esteem for *the early friend of America.*

"Permit us then to receive you as our guest; and to pay you such honors as are in our power to bestow. They are the voluntary tribute of warm and grateful hearts. We wish our children to learn, that eminent virtue affords the highest claim to honorable distinction; and that among a free people, merit will not fail of its appropriate reward.

"We beg you to accept our sincere wishes for your health and happiness, and our prayers will be offered, that your example may animate the wise and good in every nation, to contend manfully and perseveringly for the freedom and happiness of the world."

To which the General made the following reply: —

"GENTLEMEN,

"It would have been to me an inexpressible gratification on this first visit to the eastern parts of the Union, after so long an absence, to have been able to present the several towns of New-Hampshire with my personal respect, and to have witnessed the great improvement of a State, to which I am bound by early sentiments of attachment and gratitude.

"Obliged as I find myself, to take a southern course towards the seat of government, at Washington, I am happy to revisit at least the town of Portsmouth, where the remembrance of past favors, mingles with most grateful feelings for your present affectionate and flattering reception.

"I thank you, gentlemen, for your constant concern in my behalf, during the vicissitudes to which you are pleased to allude. The approbation of a free, virtuous and enlightened people, would be the highest reward for any one who knows how to value true glory; still more so, when it is bestowed on an adopted son.

"To the citizens of Portsmouth and their worthy selectmen, I offer my most respectful and affectionate acknowledgments."

Gov. Morril gave him the hearty welcome of the State, in the following address:—

"GENERAL,

"Forty years have rolled away since you left this asylum of liberty, for your native country. During this eventful period our cities have advanced, and villages have been reared; but our Langdon, our Cilley, our Poor, our Sullivan, and our Washington have passed from the stage of human action, and are gone to the land of their fathers. Although they are gone, their sons survive, and the patriotism and love of liberty which animated their breasts and excited them to those glorious acts, during our revolution, in which you, sir, shone so conspicuously, are now cherished in the bosoms of their posterity;—and we rejoice to be numbered among them;—and in the name of the patriotic citizens of New-Hampshire generally, allow me to say, that it is with no ordinary emotions we receive and welcome you to our State.

"We receive you, sir, as the friend of our nation, of liberty, and the rights of man.

"We welcome you as the magnanimous hero, who in early life, from the most pure and disinterested motives, quitted your native country, and repaired to these Colonies, then the seat of war, (contending for Independence) to embark in the struggle for the preservation of those rights, and the achievement of those privileges, which are more precious to the patriot than life itself. And, sir, it is our ardent desire, that the gratitude of Republics, but more especially of the Republic of the United States, and the smiles of Heaven, may rest upon you to the last period of your life."

The General, in his characteristic reply, alluded very affectionately to his departed associates; and the interesting changes which have taken place since he left the country. It is not necessary to add, that he expressed with emotion his acknowledgments for the cordiality of his welcome.

There was a very splendid ball in the evening, in honor of Lafayette, which he attended, and where a great number of ladies were presented to him. He left Portsmouth, 11 o'clock at night, to return to Boston, having engaged to be there on Thursday morning. While at Portsmouth he received pressing invitations to visit Exeter and Dover, but was obliged to decline them. He reached Boston about 7 o'clock, Thursday morning; and after taking some necessary repose, he received a number of revolutionary officers and soldiers; and deputations from several towns in the interior, lying on his rout to Connecticut. He then repaired to the Council Chamber, and took leave of the Governor and other members of the Supreme Executive: and afterwards set off for Lexington and Concord, and thence to Boston on his way to Worcester. He left Boston at about two o'clock, in a carriage provided by the State for his accommodation, and attended by the committee of arrangements of the city, and by the Governor's aids, who waited on him to the bounds of Connecticut. When he left the City, he expressed the gratification and delight he had experienced from the interesting recollections which had occurred to his mind, and from the great cordiality and affection with which he had been received. The Mayor assured him, that he and others were happy in the opportunity they had to manifest their attachment and respect to the early and faithful friend of the nation, and the firm and uniform friend of civil liberty.

When he passed through West Cambridge, the whole population of the town were assembled to honor the friend and guest of the nation, and to gratify their patriotic feelings by beholding this justly celebrated personage. Artillery corps stationed on the eminences adjoining the public road saluted him as he passed; and the country rung with loud huzzas and joyful acclamations. At the line of Lexington, he was received by a troop of horse and cavalcade of citizens, who conducted him into that ancient town. On his way, he passed under an arch, bearing this inscription—*"Welcome, friend of America, to the birth place of American liberty."* Salutes were again fired, and he was then conducted to the monument erected in memory of the attack of the British troops upon the militia of that place, April 19, 1775. He was here welcomed and addressed by one of the citizens in behalf of the town. Near the monument, he was introduced to *fourteen* of the militia company, which had assembled at that time, and on whom the regular troops fired, when eight of the number were slain.

After this very interesting scene, General Lafayette proceeded to Concord, and was met at the line between that place and Lexington, by a committee of the town and a respectable cavalcade of the intelligent yeomanry of the vicinity; there was also an escort composed of several companies of militia. The procession, thus formed, moved forward to the village, and the distinguished visitor was conducted to a spacious bower prepared for his reception, and tastefully decorated with evergreens and flowers by the ladies of Concord. As he entered the village, he received a salute from the artillery corps, and the vocal salutations of the inhabitants of both sexes, who had assembled to present him their grateful offerings. The peals of the village bell prolonged the acclamations of the admiring throng. The following inscription was to be seen in a conspicuous place in the arbor—*"In 1775, the people of Concord met the enemies of liberty; In 1824, they welcome the bold asserter of the rights of man, LAFAYETTE."* A sumptuous repast was provided for the occasion; and the tables were covered with all the delicacies the season and country could afford.

When General Lafayette had entered the arbor, one of the citizens addressed him by the following speech:—

"The inhabitants of Concord, by this delegation, welcome you, General, to their village. We thank you for affording us an opportunity here to offer our humble tribute of gratitude for services long since rendered, but still held in lively recollection. You, sir, now behold the *spot on which the first forcible resistance* was made to a system of measures calculated to deprive the whole people of these States of the privileges of freemen. You approved this resistance. A just estimate of the value of rational liberty led you disinterestedly, to participate with strangers in the toils, the privations, and the dangers of an arduous contest. From the 19th day of April, 1775, here noted in blood, to the memorable day in Yorktown, your heart and your sword were with us. Ten millions of grateful people now enjoy the fruits of this struggle. We can but repeat to you, sir, the cordial, affectionate, respectful welcome offered to you at your first arrival on our shores, and which we are assured will be reiterated wherever you move on American ground."

The General was, as usual, extremely happy in his reply, and alluded with sensibility to the memorable scenes of April 19, 1775.

The ladies of Concord and vicinity were present at this civic and patriotic repast; and it added much to the interest and splendour of the scene. Coffee was served up, as a counter-part of the entertainment; and Lafayette appeared to be highly pleased with the hearty reception which he met in this hospitable town. Some revolutionary characters called upon him here, who had not before seen him since he arrived; and were received with great cordiality. He spoke of the gun which had been shown him in Boston, by an inhabitant of Concord or vicinity, and which was first fired against the ministerial troops of Britain. He said, "it was the alarm gun to all Europe and to the world. For it was the signal, which summoned the civilized world to assert their rights, and to become free."

The visit at Concord was necessarily short as he had engaged to pass the night at Bolton, about twenty miles distant. He left Concord at sun-set; and was escorted on his route to Bolton, by a company of cavalry and several gentlemen of distinction belonging to that place and vicinity. He was every where greeted by the people, who collected in companies at various places, to offer him their hearty welcome. The houses on the road were illuminated, and bonfires were kindled on the adjoining hills. The militia of Bolton were assembled to receive him, though it was late in the evening when he arrived. The selectmen offered him their salutations and welcome in the name of the town. He passed the night at the hospitable mansion of Mr. W— —, where taste, variety and elegance contributed to render his reception very distinguished. Mr. W— — had resided much in France, and was particularly acquainted with Lafayette and family. Committees from Lancaster and Worcester waited on him at Bolton, to learn his plans and the probable hours of his being in those places, and to communicate the desires of the people to present him their tribute of affection and regard. He visited Lancaster early on Friday morning, where all classes of the inhabitants were assembled to bid him welcome, and to express the affectionate sentiments by which their glowing bosoms were animated. A corps of cavalry still escorted him—a national salute was fired—and the turnpike gate, at the entrance of the village, was ornamented with garlands of flowers and evergreens, and displayed this inscription, "*The* FREE *welcome the* BRAVE." He was conducted through lines formed by the citizens of both sexes, to an elevated platform, prepared in the centre of the village, and near the church; where he was addressed by the Reverend Pastor—

"General LAFAYETTE,

"In behalf of the inhabitants of Lancaster, I offer you their cordial congratulations on your arrival in a country, whose wrongs you felt and resented; whose liberties you valiantly defended; and whose interests and prospects have always been dear to your soul.

"We all unite with the few surviving veterans, who were with, loved, and respected you on the high places of the field, in giving you a welcome to this village, once the chosen residence of savages, and the scene of their most boasted triumph; and rejoice that you visit it under the improvements of civilized life, in prosperity and peace.

"It gladdens us, that we and our children may behold the man, whom we have believed, and whom we have taught them to believe, was second only to his and our friend, the immortal Washington. We participate in your joy, on beholding our institutions in vigor, our population extended, so that, since you left us, from a little one we have become millions, and from a small band a strong nation; that you see our glory rising, our republic placed on an immoveable basis, all of which are in part, under Providence, to be ascribed to your sacrifices, dangers and toils.

"We wish you health and prosperity. We assure you that wherever you shall go, you will be greeted by our fellow countrymen, as one of the chief deliverers of America, and the friend of rational liberty, and of man. It is especially our prayer, that on that day in which the acclamations and applauses of dying men shall cease to reach or affect you, you may receive from the Judge of character and Dispenser of imperishable honors, as the reward of philanthropy and incorruptible integrity, a crown of glory which shall never fade."

It is unnecessary to add, that this eloquent and pious greeting excited strong emotions in the General, and had an impressive effect on the assemblage who heard it.

The following is a report of General Lafayette's reply: —

"Accept my thanks, sir, for the kind welcome you have offered me in the name of the inhabitants of Lancaster. In returning to this country after so long an absence; in receiving such proofs of gratitude and affection wherever I go; in witnessing the prosperity of this land, — a prosperity you are pleased to say, I have been instrumental in promoting; — I feel emotions for which no language is adequate. In meeting again my former friends, in seeing the children and grand children of those who were my companions in the war of the revolution, I feel a gratification which no words can express. I beg you to accept, sir, and to offer to these people, my grateful, my affectionate acknowledgments."

In passing through Sterling and Boylston, he was saluted by the artillery companies in those respective towns, and hailed by the cordial salutations of the people, who crowded from the neighbouring country to behold the man, whom all delighted to honor. The whole population seemed to be in motion; and both old and young were eager to offer him their personal greetings. Several arches were thrown across the public road, at short notice; but indicative of the grateful dispositions of the citizens. This motto was observed on one of them—"*Welcome* LAFAYETTE, *friend of* WASHINGTON, *and adopted son of America.*"

His *entree* and reception at Worcester was highly interesting. He remained in this village several hours. The taste and wealth and patriotism of this flourishing *shire* town were unitedly and spontaneously put in requisition to prepare due honors for the "nation's guest." The number and neatness of the military, arches spacious and highly ornamented, extensive lines of the citizens and of youth expressing their gratitude in frequent and loud acclamations—all conspired to render the scene particularly brilliant. Here, as in other places, the ladies were eager to manifest the high estimation, in which they held the character of this eminent friend of liberty and virtue. He was addressed with great eloquence and feeling, by Judge Lincoln, in behalf of the citizens of the town and county of Worcester.

"GENERAL LAFAYETTE,

"The citizens whom you see assembled around you, have spontaneously thronged together, to offer you the tribute of their affection, their respect, their gratitude.

"In the name of the inhabitants of Worcester, the *shire* of an extensive county of more than 75000 population, in behalf of all who are present, and in anticipation of the commands of those, whom distance and want of opportunity occasion to be absent from this joyous scene, I repeat to you the salutations, which elsewhere have been so impressively offered upon your arrival in this country, and your visit to this Commonwealth. Welcome, most cordially welcome, to the presence of those who now greet you!

"Your name, sir, is not only associated with the memorable events of the American revolution, with the battle of Brandywine, the retreat from Valley Forge, the affair near Jamestown, and the triumph at Yorktown; but the memorials of *your* services and *our* obligations exist, in the Independence of the nation which was accomplished, in the government of the people which is established, in the institutions and laws, the arts, improvements, liberty and happiness which are enjoyed. The *sword* was beaten into the *ploughshare*, to cultivate the soil which its temper had previously defended, and the hill-tops shall now echo to the sea shore the gratulations of the independent proprietors of the land, to the common benefactor of all ranks and classes of the people.

"Wherever you go, General, the acclamations of Freemen await you — their blessings and prayers will follow you. May you live many years to enjoy the fruits of the services and sacrifices, the gallantry and valor of your earlier days, devoted to the cause of freedom and the rights of man; and may the bright examples of individual glory and of national happiness, which the history of America exhibits, illustrate to the world, the moral force of *personal* virtue, and the rich blessings of civil liberty in republican governments."

The General, in reply, said in substance, "That he received with much sensibility, the expressions of kind attention with which he was received by the inhabitants of the town and county of Worcester; that he was delighted with the fine country which he had seen, and the excellent improvement and cultivation which he witnessed; that he saw the best proofs of a great, prosperous and happy people, in the rapid advancement of the polite and useful arts, and in the stability of our free institutions; that he was especially much gratified in the great improvements of the face of the country, because he was himself a farmer; that he felt happy to observe such decided proofs of industry, sobriety and prosperity. — He begged the citizens to be assured of his affectionate and grateful recollection of their reception of him; he thanked them for all they had manifested towards him, for the kind expressions; which had been offered him by the committee, and, in a feeling impressive manner, reciprocated their good wishes."

Speaking to an individual of the attentions he had received, he observed. "It is the homage the people pay to the *principles* of the government, rather than to myself."

The inhabitants of Sturbridge and other places through which General Lafayette passed, on his way to Hartford, in Connecticut, assembled in their respective towns, and presented him the ready homage of affectionate and grateful hearts. Companies of artillery fired salutes; ladies and gentlemen gathered round him to bid him welcome to America, and to express their deep and lively sense of his past services; and many veterans of the revolutionary army pressed upon him, without ceremony or introduction, expecting, as they found, a friendly and cordial reception.

General Lafayette was received at Hartford, in Connecticut, where he arrived on Saturday morning, with similar marks of affection and esteem to those so cordially bestowed on him in the towns he had already visited. He was expected by the citizens on Friday evening, and arrangements were made for a general illumination. He was escorted into the city by the military, and a large procession of the citizens received him soon after he entered within its bounds, and conducted him to the State House, where he was addressed by the Mayor of the city, who assured him of the affectionate welcome, with which the people received him, and referred to the past services of Lafayette, which were still highly appreciated. And he expressed great happiness in beholding so many proofs of the prosperous state of the country, and in witnessing the invaluable effects of our free institutions. The greater part of the inhabitants of both sexes were personally presented to him; and there was an assemblage of children of about eight hundred, the misses all dressed in white, wearing badges with the motto, "*Nous vous aimons* LAFAYETTE." A gold medal was presented him by one of the children, which was enclosed in a paper containing these lines.

Welcome thou to freedom's clime,
Glorious Hero! Chief sublime!
Garlands bright for thee are wreath'd,
Vows of filial ardour breathed,
Veteran's cheeks with tears are wet,
"*Nous vous aimons* LAFAYETTE."

Monmouth's field is rich with bloom,
Where thy warriors found their tomb.
Yorktown's heights resound no more,
Victor's shout or cannon's roar.
Yet our hearts record their debt,
"*We do love you* LAFAYETTE."

Brandywine, whose current roll'd
Proud with blood of heroes bold,
That our country's debt shall tell,
That our gratitude shall swell,
Infant breasts thy wounds regret,
"We do love you LAFAYETTE."

Sires, who sleep in glory's bed,
Sires, whose blood for us was shed,
Taught us, when our knee we bend,
With the prayer thy name to blend;
Shall we e'er such charge forget?
No! — *"Nous vous aimons* LAFAYETTE."

When our blooming cheeks shall fade,
Pale with time, or sorrow's shade,
When our clustering tresses fair
Frosts of wintry age shall wear,
E'en till memory's sun be set,
"We will love you LAFAYETTE."

In comparison with the population of Hartford, a greater portion of his revolutionary companions were here presented to him than in any place he had visited. The number was nearly one hundred. These marched before him, in the procession, in a connected column and attended by their own music. It is hardly necessary to say, that their beloved general gave them a most cordial greeting. By one of the citizens, a sash and pair of epaulets were produced, which were worn by Lafayette when he entered the American army. The *sash was stained with blood* from his wound received in the battle of Brandywine. He left Hartford late in the afternoon, and proceeded to Middletown, where he embarked in a steam boat for New-York. The citizens of this place regretted, that he could not pass some time with them; and receive the attentions, which their grateful feelings would induce them to bestow on a zealous and able friend of American independence.

HIS RETURN TO NEW-YORK.

General Lafayette reached New-York on the following day, about noon; and was conducted to the City Hotel by the committee of arrangements, who were in waiting to receive him, when he arrived at the wharf. Multitudes assembled, who greeted his return, and renewed their joyful acclamations on meeting him again as a guest of their city. On Monday, the Cincinnati of the State of New-York gave a public dinner, in honor of "their old companion in arms," at which were also present several other persons of distinction, and the members of the City Council. This was the anniversary of the birth of Lafayette; and the circumstance increased the interesting associations of the interview. The hall of meeting was richly decorated with appropriate emblems, and portraits of some of the heroes of the revolution, and bearing the hallowed name of Washington. In the toasts given on this occasion, were illusions to the important events which occurred in the war of the revolution, and to many of the distinguished characters, who conducted it to a successful issue — Washington, Greene, Lincoln, Steuben, Knox, Gates, Clinton, Kosciusco, De Kalb, Hamilton and others.

The first volunteer toast was by the President of the Society, and was, *"Our distinguished guest;"* when a transparent painting was suddenly illuminated and unveiled, and displayed a "WELCOME;" and over the head of Lafayette a beautiful wreath of flowers was suspended. He rose and said, — "with inexpressible delight at our brotherly meeting, with my affection to you all, my very dear friends and companions in arms, I propose the following sentiment; The sacred principles for which we have fought and bled — *Liberty, equality and national independence*; may every nation of the earth in adopting them, drink a *bumper* to the old continental army." [Footnote: Some of the toasts given by General Lafayette on other occasions are here recorded, as they are indicative of the opinions and sentiments which probably predominate in his mind. At the public dinner in Boston, on the day of his arrival — "The city of Boston, the cradle of liberty; may its proud Faneuil Hall ever stand a monument to teach the world that resistance to oppression is a duty, and will, under true republican institutions, become a blessing." In the College Hall at the dinner of the Society of *Phi Beta Kappa*—"*The Holy Alliance* of virtue, literature and patriotism: It will prove too powerful for any *coalition* against the rights of man." At the military dinner on the Common in Boston, when the brilliant parade took place before mentioned—"The patriotic troops who have paraded this day, they excite the admiration of every beholder, and fill the heart with delight." At the dinner given by the citizens of Salem—"The town of Salem: may her increasing prosperity more and more evince the blessings of popular institutions, founded on the sacred basis of natural and social rights." And at Portsmouth, he gave that town, and added, "may the blessings of republican institutions furnish a refutation of the mistaken and selfish sophistry of European despotism."]

On the next day, he visited the public Schools, the College, the Hospital, and Academy of Fine Arts; and on Wednesday, embarked in a steamboat to view the fortifications in the harbor of New-York. In the evening following, he attended the theatre, and was received with universal and repeated acclamations. Many eminent persons from distant parts of the United States visited New-York, at this time, for the sole object of meeting the celebrated friend of America. Among these were Mrs. Lewis, a niece of General Washington; and Mr. Huger of South-Carolina, the brave and generous youth, who attempted the liberation of Lafayette from the dungeon of Olmutz, at the imminent hazard of his own life; and who suffered a long and severe imprisonment for his disinterested interference. He also visited the widowed ladies of Generals Montgomery and Hamilton. Of the latter general, he was the personal and ardent friend.

A public dinner was given to Lafayette by the French gentlemen resident in New-York; many of whom were among the constitutionalists in France in 1783; and who manifested equal respect and veneration for this distinguished confessor of regulated liberty, as the citizens of America. Several of the Aldermen of the city also gave splendid entertainments to the guest of the nation, who could justly claim to have acted an important part in the establishment of our freedom and independence.

He consented to attend the examination of several of the free schools—and appeared highly gratified by the evidence given of the improvement of the pupils. At one of the schools, consisting of 400 misses, after the examination, the following lines were chanted by the pupils:

Welcome, Hero, to the West,
To the land thy sword hath blest!
To the country of the *Free*,
Welcome, *Friend of Liberty*!

Grateful millions guard thy fame,
Age and youth revere thy name,
Beauty twines the wreath for thee,
Glorious *Son of Liberty*!

Tears shall speak a nation's love,
Whereso'er thy footsteps move,
By the choral *paean* met—
Welcome, welcome, Lafayette!

The *African* free school was not overlooked. While on his visit here, one of the trustees announced, that General Lafayette had been elected a member of the Manumission Society of New-York. The truly venerable John Jay is President of this benevolent association. One of the children stepped forward, and expressed their sense of the honor of the visit, and of their satisfaction in reflecting, that he was friendly to the abolition of slavery.

But the most splendid scene exhibited in this proud city, was the *fete* at Castle-garden. This was an evening party and ball, at which *six thousand* ladies and gentlemen were present. It was the most brilliant and magnificent scene ever witnessed in the United States. Castle-garden lies at a very short distance from Battery-street, which is a spacious and elegant promenade, on the south westerly part of the city. It was formerly a fort, and is about one hundred and seventy feet in diameter, of a circular or elliptical form. It has lately become a place of great resort in the warm season of the year. Everything which labor and expence, art and taste could effect was done to render it convenient, showy and elegant. An awning covered the whole area of the garden suspended at an altitude of seventy-five feet; the columns which supported the dome were highly ornamented, and lighted by an *immense* cut glass chandelier, with thirteen smaller ones appended.

The General, made his appearance about 10 o'clock; when the dance and the song was at an end. The military band struck up a grand march, and the Guest was conducted through a column of ladies and gentlemen to a splendid pavilion. Not a word was spoken of gratulation—so profound, and respectful, and intellectual was the interest which his presence excited. The interior of the pavilion which was composed of white cambric, ornamented with sky blue festoons, was richly furnished. Among other interesting objects was a bust of Hamilton, placed upon a Corinthian pillar and illuminated with a beautiful lamp. In front of the pavilion was a triumphal arch, of about 90 feet span adorned with laurel, oak, and festoons, based upon pillars of cannon fifteen feet high.—A bust of Washington, supported by a golden eagle, was placed over the arch as the presiding deity. Within the arch was a symbolic painting nearly 25 feet square, exhibiting a scroll inscribed to Fayette, with the words:—

"Honored be the faithful Patriot."

Soon after the General entered, the painting just alluded to was slowly raised, which exhibited to the audience a beautiful transparency, representing La Grange, the mansion of Lafayette. The effect was as complete as the view was unexpected and imposing. Another subdued clap of admiration followed this tasteful and appropriate and highly interesting display.

Universal harmony and good feeling prevailed; and about half past one o'clock, the General left the Castle, and embarked on board the steamboat James Kent, in his excursion up the North River, amidst renewed and prolonged acclamations. Eighty sets of cotillions were frequently on the floor at the same time.

A writer concludes the account of this fete thus; "Taking into view the immense space of the area, the gigantic ceiling of which was lined with the flags of all nations, festooned in a thousand varied shapes, and the whole most brilliantly illuminated, we can safely assert that there was never any thing to equal it in this country.

"The seats now erected around the area will accommodate about 3000 persons.

"There were 200 servants employed on this occasion, dressed in white under clothes, and blue coats, with red capes and cuffs."

He did not arrive at West-Point until about noon, having been detained some hours on the passage, by the steam boat getting on the flats in a thick fog. Before he reached this memorable spot, and as he passed near the banks of the Hudson, the people collected in great numbers, at several places, tendering him the hearty *welcome* of freemen, and expressing, by loud and long acclamations, their joy at his presence. On his arrival at West-Point, the whole establishment were in readiness to greet him. He was received under a national salute. Generals Brown and Scott of the army of the United States were also here, to bid him welcome, and bestow those honors due to the highest general officer in the national service, as well as to one who justly merited the nation's gratitude. He passed several hours at this celebrated spot; highly pleased with the appearance of the cadets, and with the evidences exhibited of improvements in military science. The recollection of times long since gone by gave a deep interest to the visit at this memorable post, some time the Head-Quarters of the American army; and the place where the infamous Arnold attempted to barter away the independence of the country. Some of the cadets wear the swords presented by Lafayette to a corps of American troops in the war of the revolution.

At a late hour in the afternoon, he proceeded up the river to Newburgh, where nearly 20,000 people were collected to greet him. They had been waiting his approach with great eagerness, and arrangements had been made to receive him with due honors, and expressive of their unbounded affection and regard. The lateness of the hour prevented their being carried into full effect. A splendid ball was given, and a sumptuous repast prepared; and he was addressed in behalf of the town, by one of the principal citizens. Arches were thrown across the principal street, and most of the buildings were illuminated. He regretted, that he had not more time at Newburgh; for this, too, is memorable as the residence of WASHING-

TON, and a part of the continental army in 1781. He embarked on board the steam boat, at twelve o'clock, and proceeded up the river, on his way to Albany. He reached Poughkeepsie at the rising of the sun. But the militia were assembled, the banks of the river, and the wharves were crowded by a happy population, impatient to present their offerings of gratitude and esteem to their heroic and benevolent visitor. Their repeated cheers made the *welkin* ring. When he landed, he was received by a battalion of the militia, in full uniform. A procession being formed, he was conducted through the most populous part of the town, to the city hotel, receiving as he passed, the constant greetings of the people.

The spacious hall in which breakfast was provided for him, was tastefully ornamented, and in various public places, inscriptions and mottos were displayed, which were expressive of the affection and respect of the inhabitants for their distinguished guest. A number of his old companions in arms were presented to him, both at this place and at Newburgh; among them was one who had served with much credit as an officer through the war, who was *ninety-five* years of age, with all his faculties unimpaired.

The reception of Lafayette at Catskill, Hudson and Livingston's manor, was highly gratifying to him, and honorable to the sensibility and patriotism of the people. He was every where met with demonstrations of joy. The overflowing gratitude, the sumptuous hospitality, the military pride, which were manifested wherever he paused, if but for an hour, were new proofs of one universal feeling of affectionate attachment to the friend of WASHINGTON and adopted son of the nation.

Very splendid preparations were made in Albany for his reception: and a great number of people had assembled from all the neighbouring towns. He did not enter the city till evening, which prevented in some measure, the brilliant honors which had been intended to be offered. A committee proceeded to meet him several miles from the city, and to conduct him on his way. They were attended by an escort of dragoons, and a great number of the citizens in carriages. The roar of cannon announced his approach, and the houses in the city were at once illuminated. The procession moved on to the capitol, amidst the cheers and *welcomes* of 40,000 people.

General Lafayette was here addressed by the mayor of the city; and being introduced to the governor, he also offered him the salutations of the state. A number of the revolutionary officers and soldiers were then presented to him. The interchange of greetings was most affectionate between the parties, and most interesting to the spectators. A standard of Gansevort's regiment, which had waved at Yorktown, under the command of Lafayette, attracted particular attention among the numerous decorations in the capitol. In the course of the evening, he was conducted to the splendid ball room, where the ladies appeared in all their attractions, and were anxious to show their respect to the far-famed hero, who almost fifty years ago, had devoted his life and his all, to the cause of America.

On the following day, many of the inhabitants of both sexes were introduced to him, at the capitol. The old soldiers of the revolution were among them. One, when he took his hand, said, "General, I owe my life to you; I was wounded at the battle of Monmouth. You visited me in the hospital—you gave me two guineas, and one to a person to nurse me. To this I owe my recovery, and may the blessing of heaven rest upon you."

He afterwards visited Troy and the great canal, recently made in the state of New-York, the commencement of which is not far from the city of Albany. He was accompanied by the governor, Hon. De Witt Clinton, the chief projector and patron of this great work, by a deputation of the city council, and several other gentlemen of distinction. When passing to the canal, he was greeted with repeated *welcomes* by the people who crowded the streets and the public roads. The steam boat which he entered, was commanded by a captain of the revolutionary army. On passing the arsenal, he was saluted by _three field pieces captured at *Yorktown*. Here he was also shown the field train taken from *Burgoyne*, and some French field pieces which he was instrumental in procuring to be sent to the United States, in 1779. At Troy, he was received by a deputation of the city, and one of them addressed him in the name of the inhabitants; referring to his meritorious services, and declaring the joy they experienced in beholding him in this favoured land of peace and freedom. He also received an affectionate address from the Free Masons, and one still more affectionate from the ladies of Troy. They bid him *welcome*, and acknowledged that to him, with others, they were indebted for the blessings of social, and the joys of domestic life. The misses of the academy were then presented to him, and sang a hymn prepared for the occasion. He made a short reply, but was so much affected, that it was not sufficiently understood to be preserved. He then returned to Albany, followed by the cheers and blessings of the people, who crowded about him on the water and on the land.

In the evening he embarked on board a steamboat for the city of New-York, "amidst the melody of music, the shouts of the people, and the roar of cannon." His departure excited deep regret, but it was matter of joy, that they had had opportunity to present their offerings of respect, to such a pre-eminent friend of America.

In the winter of 1777-8, General Lafayette was a short time at Albany, as commander of the troops stationed in than quarter, after the capture of Burgoyne. There was a plan in contemplation at this time, to make an attack upon Canada, but it was not prosecuted. The recollection of this circumstance, no doubt, added to the pleasure which swelled the joyful hearts of the good people of Albany. For his conduct in that department, as well as on all other occasions, manifested his great regard for the comfort and the improvement of the soldiers. When he first arrived, he was not very cordially received; he was young, being then only about twenty; and they were full of respect also for their victorious general Gates. But his attention was immediately given to improve the condition of the troops; he was constant in his personal anxiety to provide clothes, provisions and comfortable quarters for them, of which they were sadly deficient. He visited the hospital, and furnished cordials for the sick, from his own private resources; and was also duly careful of the discipline and order of those, who were able to perform military duty. The feeling of the soldiers was soon changed; they became personally and warmly attached to him, in a short time, and many, at this day, have a deep and grateful remembrance of his kindness as a man, as well as of his fidelity and energy as an officer.

General Lafayette passed three days in the city of New-York, on his return from Albany. The society of Free Masons gave him a public dinner, which was uncommonly sumptuous and splendid, and the mayor of the city entertained him with distinguished hospitality. Wherever he appeared, many of the citizens attended him, and all expressed their joy at his presence. One of them presented him a cane, worn by FRANKLIN, and left in his will to Washington.

He left New-York on Thursday, the 23d of September, attended by a deputation of the city and the Society of Cincinnati. When he reached the shore of New Jersey, the Governor of that state was ready to receive him. He bid him welcome in the name of the state, and offered him his own cordial salutations. He was conducted on his way by squadrons of horse, and a large cavalcade of the citizens, and his progress was announced by frequent salutes. His reception at Newark was unusually splendid; three thousand infantry and five hundred cavalry were paraded and reviewed by him. A spacious bower was prepared to receive him, which was highly ornamented, and he was addressed by the Attorney General of the state. After partaking of a collation, he proceeded for Elizabethtown, accompanied by the governor, with a military escort. A procession of the citizens was formed to receive and conduct him into the centre of the city; arches and bowers were erected, military parade exhibited, salutes were fired, and bells were ringing; the people cheered, the ladies welcomed him; collations were prepared, and public officers were eager in their attentions and assiduities.

Pursuing his route towards Philadelphia, he reached *New Brunswick* the next day, and the day following, arrived at *Princeton*. He was detained on his way, at several places, by the earnest solicitations of the people, who were desirous of manifesting the grateful sense they cherished of his meritorious services and exalted worth. At Princeton, he was met by a deputation from *Trenton*, a place rendered memorable by the victory which General Washington obtained over a large body of the British troops in December, 1776, when he had under his command a much smaller number, many of which were militia. He was escorted to that place by the citizens and a company of cavalry, as in other parts of his journey. When he arrived, he was addressed by the mayor, in a very affectionate manner. We can only furnish the following extract: —

"To receive upon this spot, where your Friend, our illustrious WASHINGTON, raised the first successful barrier against the relentless tide of oppression, which, in the eventful period of seventy-six, was rolling over our country; the hero who, in the succeeding stages of our revolutionary struggle, acted so conspicuous a part, and contributed so essentially to its glorious termination, cannot fail to awaken the most agreeable sensations. Next to our beloved Washington, there is no name entwined with deeper interest in the hearts of Jerseymen, than LAFAYETTE—None, which they will transmit to their posterity, encircled with a wreath of nobler praise, or embalmed with the incense of purer love, than that of the interesting stranger who embarked his life and fortune open the tempestuous ocean of our revolution—and who fought at Brandywine, at Monmouth and at Yorktown, to procure for Americans, those blessings you now see them so fully, and we trust, so gratefully enjoy."

The following is the General's answer to the address at Princeton:—

"GENTLEMEN,

"While the name of this city recalls important military remembrance, it is also connected with that of the illustrious college, which, in diffusing knowledge and liberal sentiments, has greatly contributed to turn those successes to the advantage of public liberty. Your library had been destroyed; but your principles were printed in the hearts of American patriots. I feel much obliged, sir, to your kind recollection of the diploma, which the signature of my respected friend Doctor Witherspoon, renders still more precious to me; and I beg you, gentlemen, and you, interesting grand sons of my contemporary friends, to accept my affectionate acknowledgments."

The civic arch reared at Trenton to his honor was the same, which 35 years before, was erected to receive the revered Washington.—A sumptuous dinner was served up to him, his family, and the deputations which attended on him. He spent the evening with his brother-soldiers of the Cincinnati, and other revolutionary worthies.

On the Sabbath he attended divine service in the forenoon, and visited Joseph Bonaparte in the afternoon. The latter apologized for not making the first call, on the ground that it would necessarily involve him in public associations, which it was his duty and his wish to avoid. —He added, "*I am in adversity and misfortune — You, General, are full of honor and glory, and deserving of both.*"

After passing the Delaware, thirty miles from Philadelphia, he was met by the Governor of Pennsylvania and suite, with an escort of two hundred and fifty cavalry. For his accommodation, a splendid barouche was provided, drawn by six cream coloured lofty steeds. "The guest of the nation entered its former capitol" about noon, on Tuesday, the 28th of September. When the Governor met Lafayette, as above mentioned, he welcomed him to the State in the following address: —

"GENERAL LAFAYETTE,

"The citizens of Pennsylvania behold, with the most intense feeling and exalted regard, the illustrious friend and companion of Washington.

"With sentiments of the highest veneration and gratitude, we receive the early and great benefactor of the United States; the enlightened statesman, philanthropist and patriot of both hemispheres.

"The sincere and universal joy which your arrival has diffused over the nation, is no where more deeply or enthusiastically felt, than in Pennsylvania; whose fields and streams are rendered memorable by your achievements; whose citizens were the followers of your standard, and the witnesses of your sacrifices and toils, in the defence of American liberty. The eventful scenes of your useful life are engraved on our hearts. A nation has rejoiced at your successes, and sympathized with your sorrows.

"With ardent pleasure we have ever observed your strenuous exertions as the friend of man; and whilst your great services, rendered in the cause of humanity, have commanded our admiration, the purity of your motives has insured the love and affection of Americans.

"With the best feelings of the heart we now approach you, with the assurance that, if any thing could add to our happiness on this interesting occasion, it would be the hope of enjoying the distinguished honor of your permanent residence among us, and that a long and splendid life of usefulness may be closed in the State, whose soil has been moistened with your blood, generously shed in the cause of virtue, liberty and independence."

Answer of General Lafayette.

"On the happy moment, long and eagerly wished for, when I once more tread the soil of Pennsylvania, I find in her affectionate welcome, so kindly expressed by her first magistrate, a dear recollection of past favors and a new source of delightful gratifications. The very names of this state and her capitol, recall to the mind those philanthropic and liberal sentiments, which have marked every step of their progress.

"Pennsylvania has been the theatre of most important events; a partaker in the arduous toils and meritorious sacrifices, which insured the success of our glorious and fruitful revolution, I particularly thank you, sir, for your gratifying mention of my personal obligations to the Pennsylvanian line; nor will I ever forget, that on Pennsylvania ground, not far from this spot, I enjoyed, for the first time, the delight to find myself under American tents, and in the family of our beloved commander in chief. Now, sir, Pennsylvania is in full possession, and reaps all the prosperities and happy consequences of that great national union, of those special institutions, which by offering in a self-governed people the most perfect example of social order that ever existed have reduced to absurdity and ridicule the anti-popular arguments of pretended statesmen in other countries. In whatever way I may he disposed of by the duties and feelings, in which you have been pleased to sympathise, I shall ever rank this day among the most fortunate of my life; and, while I beg you, sir, personally to accept my cordial acknowledgements, I offer through you a tribute of profound gratitude and respectful devotion to the citizens of Pennsylvania."

His entrance into the fair city, founded by the wise and benevolent *Penn*, is described as most magnificent in all its accompaniments. The population poured forth to meet him at an early hour. Carriages, horsemen and pedestrians filled every avenue for a distance of five miles; and the windows and stagings were thronged with ladies eager to welcome him. Just at the entrance of the city, a division of militia, composed of cavalry, artillery and infantry was drawn up in a hollow square, on a piece of land of about forty acres, to receive the Patriot Hero, whose approach was announced by a salute of 100 rounds of artillery. Lafayette, uncovered and standing up in the barouche, was seen by the whole field. The car of Saladin could not have exceeded that of Lafayette. The troops were nearly six thousand. After the review, which the general made on foot, he received the saluting honors in his barouche.

The line of march into the city was then taken up. It extended nearly three miles, and passed through numerous streets. More than six hours were consumed in proceeding from Frankfort to the State House, a distance of about four miles. A full description of the procession, and the decorated arches, &c. under which it passed, would occupy too great a portion of this volume—we can only give the outline of the procession.

A cavalcade of 100 citizens preceded; followed by 100 general, field and staff officers. Then came a *square* of cavalry; a band of music, mounted, and a corps of 160 cavalry. Next a brigade of infantry, with flank companies.

Committee of arrangements. General Lafayette and Judge Peters, in the splendid barouche.

Then followed four other barouches, drawn by four horses each, with Governors Shulze and Williamson, and suites, the general's family, and distinguished individuals.

Then three cars, of large dimensions, containing 120 revolutionary heroes and worthies, each car characteristically decorated; bearing on their front "WASHINGTON," on the rear "LAFAYETTE," and on the sides, "*defenders of our country,*" "*The survivors of 1776.*"

Then advanced 400 young men. After these the procession of trades, led by a car, containing a body of printers at work at case and press—the latter striking off, and distributing, copies of an ode on the occasion—followed by the typographical society, with a banner, with the inscription: "LAFAYETTE—_the friend of universal liberty, and the rights of the *press.*"

Then followed 200 cordwainers (with banners, badges, emblems, &c. The other trades were also decorated;)—300 weavers;—150 ropemakers;—150 lads, uniformly dressed;—100 shipbuilders;—700 mechanics of different professions, not enumerated;—150 coopers, with a car containing a cooper's shop, the workmen fitting staves and driving hoops:—Then came 150 butchers, well mounted and neatly dressed in their frocks;—then 260 carmen, mounted, with aprons trimmed with blue; and a body of 150 riflemen, in frocks, dressed with plaids, leopard skins, &c. A company of artillery, with two pieces; a brigade of infantry and the New Jersey cavalry. A body of 300 farmers closed the procession.

Besides the above, there were the Red Men of the state, the Lafa-
yette
Association, the True Republican Society, the Washington and
Lafayette
Society; and the German American Society.

The appearance of the whole of this truly grand procession was august and imposing. As it passed, Lafayette! Lafayette! sprang from the voices of a multitude that rolled on, and on, and on, like wave after wave of the ocean, in numbers we shall not presume to name, (but which were estimated at 200,000.) Lafayette beat in every heart—Lafayette hung on every tongue—Lafayette glowed on every cheek—Lafayette glistened on every swimming eye—Lafayette swelled on every gale. The whole city and country appeared to have arrayed themselves in all their glory, and beauty, and strength, at once to witness and adorn the majesty of the spectacle; and the fash-ionable part of the community seemed determined to exhibit the perfection of taste in the beauty of the decoration of their persons, and the richness of their attire. In Chestnut-street wreathes were cast into the barouche, as it passed, and many of them were from the fairbands of Quakeresses.

After the procession had passed through the principal streets, the front halted at the old State-House, which contains the hall in which the *Declaration of Independence* was signed in 1776.

Here the general alighted, passed under a most magnificent tri-umphal arch, and was conducted to the hall, which is 40 feet square and was decorated in the most splendid manner. Among the decorations was a statue of Washington, and portraits of William Penn, Franklin, Robert Morris, Francis Hopkinson, Greene, Wayne, Montgomery, Hamilton, Gates, Rochambeau, Charles Carrot, M'Kean, Jefferson, Hancock, Adams, Madison, Monroe, and Charles Thompson.— The portrait of Washington, by Peale, occupied the first place, and was the most splendidly decorated. Here were assembled the city authorities, the society of Cincinnati, the judges, officers of the army and navy, and the committee of arrangements, all seated on superb sofas.

The Governor of the State having been presented, General Lafayette, Judge Peters, and George Washington Lafayette were introduced, the company all standing. The Mayor of the city then welcomed the guest, in the following address:—

"GENERAL,

"The citizens of Philadelphia welcome to their homes, the Patriot who has long been dear to their hearts.

"Grateful at all times for the enjoyment of a free government, they are, on this occasion, peculiarly anxious but unable to express a deep felt sentiment of pure affection toward those venerated men whose martial and civil virtues, under Providence, have conferred upon themselves and their descendents, this mighty blessing.

"Forty-eight years ago, in this city, and in this hallowed hall, which may emphatically be called the *birth place of independence*, a convention of men, such as the world has rarely seen, pre-eminent for talents and patriotism, solemnly declared their determination to assume for themselves the right of self-government; and that they and their posterity should thence forth assert their just rank among the nations of the earth. A small, but cherished band of those who breasted the storm and sustained the principles thus promulgated to the world, still remains—In the front rank of these worthies, history will find, and we now delight to honor, General Lafayette, whose whole life has been devoted to the cause of freedom and to the support of the inalienable rights of man.

"General—Many of your co patriots have passed away, but the remembrance of their virtues and their services, shall never pass from the minds of this people; their's is an imperishable fame, the property of ages yet to come. But we turn from the fond recollection of the illustrious dead to hail with heart-felt joy the illustrious living, and again bid welcome, most kindly and affectionately welcome, to the guest of the nation, the patriot Lafayette."

The general made the following answer:

"My entrance through this fair and great city, amidst the most solemn and affecting recollections, and under all the circumstances of a welcome which no expression could adequately acknowledge, has excited emotions in my heart, in which are mingled the feelings of nearly fifty years.

"Here, sir, within these sacred walls, by a council of wise and devoted patriots, and in a style worthy of the deed itself, was boldly declared the independence of these vast United States, which, while it anticipated the independence, and I hope, the *republican* independence, of the whole American hemisphere, has begun, for the civilized world, the era of a new and of the only true social order founded on the unalienable rights of man, the practicability and advantages of which are every day admirably demonstrated by the happiness and prosperity of your populous city.

"Here, sir, was planned the formation of our virtuous, brave, revolutionary army, and the providential inspiration received, that gave the command of it to our beloved, matchless Washington. But these and many other remembrances, are mingled with a deep regret for the numerous cotemporaries, for the great and good men whose loss we have remained to mourn.—It is to their services, sir, to your regard for their memory to your knowledge of the friendships I have enjoyed, that I refer the greater part of honors here and elsewhere received, much superior to my individual merit.

"It is also under the auspices of their venerated names, as well as under the impulse of my own sentiments, that I beg you Mr. Mayor, you gentlemen of both councils, and all the citizens of Philadelphia, to accept the tribute of my affectionate respect and profound gratitude."

General Lafayette remained in Philadelphia a week; and the repeated and constant attentions shown him by public societies and by distinguished individuals, were such as might have been expected from the celebrated hospitality and civism of that city, and such as was not unworthy of their eminent guest. The governor of the state was attentive and courteous to him during his whole visit; and other public functionaries, both civil and military, were eager of the honor of manifesting their great respect for his character. That portion of the citizens, who belong to the religious society of Friends, appeared equally cordial and happy in an opportunity to assure him of their esteem. It is not consistent with their principles to make a great parade, or to prepare expensive and useless ceremonies. They did not all approve of the plan of illumination. In the wish to have it general, some ardent citizens censured the *friends* for declining to do it—But this was a mistaken zeal. The religious opinions and conscientious scruples of all classes of people are entitled to respect. It would have been altogether unjustifiable, had there been an attempt to force the *friends* into the measure. They are a very respectable class of citizens; and we trust, that for no purposes of parade or ceremony, they will ever be required to violate their consciences, or be subjected to insult for any non-compliance. The following lines were written by one of that religious society, on the occasion, and cannot fail to be acceptable to every liberal mind.

TO LAFAYETTE.

O! think not our hearts void of gratitude's glow,
  For the friend of our country, for *liberty's friend*,
Tho' we do not with others loud praises bestow,
  The kind hand of friendship we freely extend.

We welcome thee back to the land where thy name,
  In boyhood we lisp'd, and in manhood revere;
Tho' we bind not thy brows with the chaplet of fame,
  Accept, beloved guest, a warm tribute—a tear!

Yes—a tear of affection which starts to the eye,
  When tracing thy storm-beaten pathway through life;

That thy principles pure could ambition defy,
  Thy humanity prompt thee to stay the fierce strife.

In thee we behold not the chieftain whose sword
  Delighting in bloodshed is ever unsheath'd;
But the friend of mankind, whose mild actions afford
  A proof that his lips no hypocrisy breath'd.

Then welcome once more to the land where thy name
  In boyhood we lisp'd, and in manhood revere;
Tho' we twine not thy brows with the war-wreath of fame,
  Accept, beloved guest, a warm tribute — A TEAR.

While in Philadelphia, General Lafayette visited the navy yard. The Governor accompanied him in this visit, and he was also attended by a large escort and procession. He was addressed by commodore Barron, in a very appropriate and feeling manner. A great number of ladies were presented to him at the commodore's quarters. On his return, he attended a splendid entertainment provided for him by the Free Masons. A ball was also given in honor of Lafayette, while he was in Philadelphia, the must brilliant and the most numerous ever known in the city. The Miss Bollmans, daughters of Dr. Bollman, who generously attempted the rescue of Lafayette from the prison at Olmutz, were present. On one day, 2000 children assembled at the State House to be presented to him; and one of them addressed him. The scene was said to be uncommonly interesting. — The following was his reply to the address of the Frenchmen in Philadelphia: —

"MY DEAR COUNTRYMEN,

"Amidst the enjoyments with which my heart is filled in this happy country, I experience a very great one in seeing myself surrounded by the testimonies of your friendship. It was in the hall in which now receive you, that the sacred sovereignty of the people was recognized by a French Minister, eleven years before it was proclaimed on the 11th of July, 1789, in the bosom of the Constituent Assembly. You are right in thinking that this first impulse of 1789, has, notwithstanding our misfortunes, greatly meliorated the situation of the French people. I participate in your wishes and your hopes for the freedom of our country. This hope is well founded, these wishes will be fulfilled. In the mean while I am happy in tendering to you this day the expression of my lively gratitude and tender affection."

We give here also the address of Captain Barron to Lafayette, when he visited the navy yard near Philadelphia:—

"GENERAL LAFAYETTE,

"To receive you at this naval station with the highest honors, is not less in obedience to our instructions, than to the impulse of our hearts.

"We rejoice in the opportunity of testifying to you, and to the world, our gratitude to one distinguished among that band of glorious heroes, to whom we are indebted for the privilege we now enjoy.

"You, sir, whose whole life has been devoted to the extension of civil liberty, must at this period be enriched by feelings which rarely fall to the lot of man.

"Turning from the old world, whose excesses have been almost fatal to the cause of liberty, to the new, where that cause has prospered to an unexampled degree, you see a proof, that political liberty is not visionary.

"The soldier will here behold the nation for which he has fought, not exhausted by his triumphs, nor sacrificed to idle ambition, but raised by his valor to liberty and independence; and while enjoying these blessings themselves, securing them for the remotest posterity.

"The patriot will here see a people, not distracted by faction, nor yet regardless of their political rights, making the most rapid strides to true greatness, and displaying in their happiness and security, the wisdom and power of institutions engraved on their hearts.

"To you, sir, the soldier and patriot, we offer this cheering picture; and if ever you can be recompensed for your generous devotion to us in our revolutionary struggle, it must be in the pleasure with which you witness our national happiness.

"Permit me then, dear General, to assure you that among the ten millions that bid you welcome, none do it with more sincerity than those of the navy."

Answer of General Lafayette.

"The extraordinary honors of which an American veteran is now the happy object, I consider as being shared in common with my surviving companions; and for the greater part, bestowed as an approbation of the principle, and a tribute of regard, to the memory of the illustrious patriots with whom I have served in the cause of America and mankind.

"It is with the most lively feelings of an American heart, that I have sympathised in all the circumstances relative to the United States' Navy, and proudly gloried in the constant superiority of the American flag over an enemy, justly renowned for bravery and maritime skill.

"I am happy, my dear Commodore, in your affectionate welcome; but whatever may be my feelings of personal gratitude to the Navy of the United States, I feel myself under still greater obligations to them, for the honor they have done to the American name in every part of the globe."

The 5th of October, Lafayette left Philadelphia, on this journey to the south, by the way of Wilmington, Baltimore and Washington. He passed the Brandywine, and entered Wilmington, the capital of Delaware, on the 6th about noon. He was received with demonstrations of lively gratitude and joy; and a sumptuous repast was provided for him. He then proceeded to Newcastle in that state, and was present at the marriage of Colonel V. Dupont, formerly one of his aids in France. From this place he proceeded to Frenchtown, where he was received by the aids of the Governor of Maryland, with a battalion of horse as an escort for their honorable guest. He was waited on, also, by deputations both civil and military, from

the city of Baltimore, each of which offered him their cordial salutations in the name of those whom they represented. General Harper
was at the head of the military deputation; and having given him a
hearty welcome, introduced his Brother officers, amounting to two
hundred. Several revolutionary officers and soldiers, who had repaired to this place for the pleasure of an early meeting, were also
introduced to him. The joy of the meeting was reciprocal. Among
the many former personal friends, he met here with M. Du Bois
Martin, who procured the ship in which Lafayette first came to
America in 1777. The interview must have been extremely interesting.

Lafayette embarked at Frenchtown in the steamboat United
States, for Baltimore, furnished for his accommodation by that city.
On his arrival in the river, columns of smoke in the direction of
Baltimore, announced to those on board, the approach of a squad-
ron of steam boats; and in three quarters of an hour the Virginia, the
Maryland, the Philadelphia, &c. swept gallantly by, two on either
side, crossed immediately under the stern of the United States, and
took their positions *en echellon*. The Maryland and Virginia then
came close along side, their decks crowded with spectators, who
saluted the General with continued shouts. The whole fleet then
proceeded slowly up the river, all elegantly decorated with flags
closed into the centre as it passed the narrows opposite Fort M'Henry, and dropt anchor, forming a semi-circle near the northern shore.

Just as the anchor was let go a signal gun was fired, and a squad
ron of eight green and white barges, which had been awaiting the
coming of Lafayette, shot across the bows of the United States, and
passing round in regular order under the stern, came along side to
receive the passengers. The first was handsomely carpeted and
cushioned, manned by masters of vessels, and intended for Lafayette.

The General embarked in this boat amidst the repeated cheering
of all around, and pushing off made way for the others, which took
on board the committees and proceeded in order to the wharf.

The General was received on the way by the commander of the
garrison, and proceeded to the star fort. The Governor of the State
was here introduced to the General, who addressed him, to which

the General made a feeling reply. He was afterwards conducted to the tent of Washington by Governor Stevens, within which he was received by the society of Cincinnati. The scene was impressive. As soon as the first emotions had subsided, the hero of the Cowpens, Colonel Howard, President of the society, addressed the General, who, in reply, said language could not express his feelings. He then embraced his old companions in arms. The General and invited guests then retired to an adjoining marquee, and took refreshments; after which he was seated in an elegant barouche, attended by Mr. Carroll, and Generals Smith and Howard, drawn by four black horses, with two postillions in white silk jackets, blue sashes and black velvet caps, led by four grooms similarly dressed. At the outer gate, the procession was received by about 1000 cavalry. On passing Federal Hall, a salute was fired. Descending the hall, the procession passed under an elegant arch, and another at the head of Market-street, where his friends left the carriage, and the General alone proceeded down the military line, in presence of thousands of both sexes.

After this he descended at the Exchange, where he was received by the Mayor and Councils, with an appropriate address and answer. He thence proceeded in his carriage to Light-street, across which, at the entrance into Market- street, an elegant pavilion had been erected, and where he was received by a fine military assemblage. Here there was a truly splendid ceremony, in presentment by the Mayor, to the General, with Pulaski's standard, made during the revolutionary war by a Moravian Nun, at Bethlehem, Pennsylvania, which belonged to Pulaski's legion, raised in Baltimore in 1778. In 1779, Count Pulaski was mortally wounded at the attack on Savannah; and these colors, at his decease, in 1780, descended to the Major, who was sabred to death in South Carolina. The venerable Paul Bentalou, Esq. now marshal of the district of Maryland, and at that time captain of the first troop of light dragoons, and senior surviving officer, inherited the standard of the legion, which he has preserved with Great care to this day, with all the fond recollections and attachments of the veteran soldier.

In the evening, the city was brilliantly illuminated, and many of the public and private buildings exhibited appropriate transparencies.

On Friday, hundreds of citizens were presented to the General, in the Hall of the Exchange; and in the afternoon he dined with the Mayor and Corporation. In the evening, he attended the ball and supper given to him by the citizens, which was truly splendid, and occupies many columns in the description.

The General was also waited upon, and addressed in the most feeling manner, by the French residents, to whom he replied in the most affectionate manner.

At seven o'clock in the evening the General was received at Masonic Hall, by the Grand Lodge of Maryland, in the presence of eight hundred brethren, The General dined with the Cincinnati on Saturday. "On Monday he was presented with a medal from the young men of Baltimore, with inscriptions expressive of their gratitude. He afterwards presented several colors to the fifth regiment, under Colonel Stewart, in his behalf, which were received with the highest military honors. The General then reviewed the regiment. — At eleven o'clock he left his lodgings, and proceeded in his barouche to Whetstom Point, for the purpose of reviewing the third division, under the command of Major General Harper. He partook of a splendid military banquet. His honors on leaving the city were magnificent as those of his reception. He departed under escort on Monday, over the Washington turnpike. He was to pass the night 30 miles from Baltimore, and enter Washington city on Tuesday at noon."

In no city which General Lafayette visited, had he met with a more cordial welcome, or a more splendid reception, than in Baltimore. All were desirous to do him honor and to express their feelings of gratitude and respect for the guest of the nation. Many interesting recollections must have been brought to his mind when in this city. It was here he passed some time in 1781, when he commanded the American light infantry in that quarter — when the British had a large army in the vicinity, and our troops were destitute of clothing, and in a state of great despondence. By his own personal influence and responsibility, he obtained a loan here for the use of his troops, which was necessary to their comfort, and served to render them in a measure contented with their situation. The address of his old friend Colonel Howard, in behalf of the Cincinnati of Maryland, who were assembled in the Tent of Washington to receive his adopted son, and their beloved brother soldier, was as follows: —

"GENERAL,

"A few of your brother soldiers of Maryland, who remain after a lapse of forty years, and the sons of some of them who are now no more, are assembled in the Tent of Washington, to greet you on your visit to the United States; and to assure you of their affectionate and sincere regard. This Tent will call to your recollection many interesting incidents which occurred when you associated in arms with Washington, the patriot and soldier, saviour of his country, and friend of your youth.

"Accept, General, our cordial sentiments of esteem for you, and of gratitude for services rendered by you to our country — services which will never be forgotten by the free and happy people of the United States."

To which General Lafayette replied —

"The pleasure to recognize my beloved companions in arms; the sound of names, whose memory is dear to me; this meeting under the consecrated *Tent*, where we so often pressed around our paternal commander in chief; excite emotions which your sympathizing hearts will better feel than I can express. This post also nobly defended in the late war, while it brings the affecting recollection of a confidential friend in my military family, associates with the remembrance of the illustrious defence of another fort, in the war of the revolution, by the *friend* now near me. [Colonel Smith.] It has been the lot of the Maryland line, to acquire glory in instances of bad as well as of good fortune; and to whom can I better speak of that glory, than in addressing Colonel Howard? My dear brother soldiers, my feelings are too strong for utterance. I thank you most affectionately."

The meeting of this Society was rendered peculiarly interesting, — there being present, besides many other worthy veterans of the revolutionary army, Colonel John F. Howard, the celebrated hero of the battle of the Cowpens, January 1781, to whom Congress presented two medals, in testimony of his singular bravery-General (formerly Colonel) Samuel Smith, who bravely defended Mud-fort, and many years senator in Congress; and Paul Bentalou, Esq. now marshal of Maryland district, who was the senior captain of light dragoons, belonging to Pulaski's legion, in 1778. Here also the very venerable Charles Carroll, one of the signers of the declaration of independence, was introduced to Lafayette.

We give also an extract from the address of Governor Stevens, to the General.

"SIR,

"In bidding you a hearty welcome to the state of Maryland, whilst I gratify the feelings of my own heart, I express, though feebly, those of the people, whom it is my pride and pleasure, on this occasion to represent. Beneath this venerable canopy, many a time have you grasped the friendly hand of our illustrious Washington, aided his council with your animating voice, or shared with him the hardy soldier's meal. The incidents which the association so forcibly recalls, however inspiring, it were needless to dwell upon. The recollection of them fills the mind with gratitude; a full measure of which is justly due to you, as the generous companion of our fathers, the gallant and disinterested soldier of liberty — You are about to enter the city of Baltimore, which you have known in other days. In her growth and embellishment, you will behold a symbol of our national prosperity, under popular institutions and a purely representative government. — Welcome, thrice welcome, General, to the soil of Maryland. Nothing which we can do, can too strongly express to you the affection and respect which we entertain for your person and your principles, or the joy with which we receive you among us, as a long absent father on a visit to his children."

To this address Lafayette replied —

"While your Excellency is pleased so kindly to welcome me in the name of the citizens of Maryland, the lively gratitude, which this most gratifying reception cannot fail to excite, associates in my heart, with a no less profound sense of my old obligations to this state, both as an American General and a personal friend. I am happy, sir, to have the honor to meet you in this fort, so gallantly defended in the late war, in presence of the brave colonel of the worthy volunteers, whose glory on that occasion I have enjoyed with the proud feelings of an American veteran. It was by a Maryland colonel in the year 1777, that the British received, in the gallant defence of an important fort, one of the first lessons of what they were to expect from American valour and patriotism. The Maryland line, sir, in the continental army has been conspicuous, not only in days of victory, but on days either unfortunate or dubious. This tent, under which I now answer your affectionate address; the monument erected to the memory of our great and good commander in chief; the column of a later date, bearing testimonies of a glorious event; my entrance into a city long ago dear to me, and now become so beautiful and prosperous; fill my heart with sentiments, in which you have had the goodness to sympathize.

"Accept, sir, the tribute of my respectful and affectionate gratitude to the citizens of the state, and their honored chief magistrate."

There was an incident connected with General Lafayette's escort to the boundary of Baltimore, which deserves to be particularly noticed. The cavalry troop was commanded by Samuel Sprigg, Esq. who, two years ago, ended a full term of service in the capacity of Governor of the state of Maryland, of which he was Captain-General and Commander in Chief. Returned to private life, a wealthy planter, in the midst of all that can render life easy and pleasant, he is proud of resuming his character of a citizen, and becoming a member of a troop of horse, in which he enrolls himself with his neighbours, who choose him their commander. In that capacity, he has had the pleasure of receiving General Lafayette at the boundary of his county, and escorting him through it. This incident, we say, deserves to be noted as a fine practical illustration of the principles of republican government.

General Lafayette arrived in the city of Washington, according to previous arrangement, about 1 o'clock on Tuesday the 12th.

About 9 o'clock, on Tuesday morning, the General and suit left Rossburg, and proceeded to the District of Columbia, at the line of which he was met by the committee of arrangements from the city of Washington, and a number of revolutionary officers, escorted by a handsome troop of city cavalry, and a company of Montgomery cavalry. The meeting of the General with his revolutionary compatriots, and with the committee, was affectionate and impressive in the extreme. After many embraces were exchanged, the General was transferred to the elegant landau provided by the city for his use, drawn by four fine greys, in which he was accompanied by Major General Brown and Commodore Tingey, members of the committee; and his son George Washington Lafayette, his Secretary, Col. Vassieur, and Mr. Custis, of Arlington, were placed in another carriage provided for the purpose. The whole then advanced to the city, Capt. Sprigg's company in front, the remaining companies proceeding and flanking the carriages containing the General, his suite, the committee, &c. On rising to the extensive plain which stretches eastward from the capitol to the Anacosta river, the General found himself in front of the most brilliant military spectacle which our city ever witnessed, being a body of 10 or 1200 troops, composed entirely of volunteer companies of the city, Georgetown, and Alexandria, some of them recently organized, clad in various tasteful uniforms, and many of them elegant beyond any thing of the kind we have before seen. Brigadier Generals Smith and Jones were in the field with their respective suits and the field officers of the first brigade. These troops, together with the large body of cavalry, the vast mass of eager spectators which overspread the plain, and the animation of the whole, associated with the presence of the venerated object of so much curiosity and affection, gave a grandeur and interest to the scene which has never been equaled here on any former occasion. After the General had received the respects and welcome of our military chiefs, the whole body of troops tools took up the escort, for the capitol, wheeling into column, in East Capitol-street, and then into linc upon the leading division. The General and suite then passed this line in review, advancing towards the capitol, and receiving the highest military honors as he passed.

After the military procession had reached the east end of the market house, on East Capitol-street, which was handsomely adorned with proper emblems, and the Declaration of Independence, above which perched a living eagle of the largest size, the committee of arrangements and General Lafayette and suite alighted from their carriages and preceded by the committee, the General and suite passed through the market house, which on each side was lined with anxious and delighted spectators, to the east entrance of the Capitol Square, over which was thrown a neat arch, decorated with evergreens and other ornaments, with appropriate labels, expressive of the esteem and gratitude of the citizens to the national guest; on the pinnacle stood another eagle. On entering the gate, the General was met by a group of 25 young girls, dressed in white, intended to represent the 24 States and the District of Columbia, each wearing a wreath of flowers, and bearing in her hand a miniature national flag, with the name of one of the States inscribed upon it; when the one representing the district advanced and arrested his progress, and, in a short speech, neatly and modestly delivered their welcome to the nation's guest. After which each of the young ladies presented her hand to the General, which he received in the most affectionate manner, and with the kindest expressions. He then passed a double line of girls, properly dressed, from the schools, who strewed his way with flowers. Leaving the girls, he passed lines of the students of the colleges and seminaries, with their respective banners, and a company of Juvenile Infantry, dressed in uniform, and armed in a suitable manner; and then the younger boys from the schools. All these formed a numerous and highly interesting assemblage. Arriving at the north wing of the Capitol, the General was conducted by the committee of arrangements through the great door, up the grand staircase, into the central rotunda of the Capitol, which though of immense size, was filled with ladies and gentlemen; and, through it, received, on every side, demonstrations of the most ardent and grateful respect. On leaving the rotunda, he passed under the venerable tent of Washington, also filled with ladies, revolutionary officers, and other gentlemen, to the front of the portico of the Capitol, neatly carpeted, on which was erected the tent. He was introduced to the Mayor, who introduced him to the Mayor of Georgetown, the members of the corporation, and other gentlemen present, when advancing to the front of the portico, in the presence of many thousand spectators, the Mayor delivered an address, to which the General replied.

The General was then invited by the Mayor of Georgetown to visit that town, in a chaste and neat address.

To which the General replied, in a few words, that Georgetown was an old acquaintance of his, where he had found many valuable and esteemed friends, and he would visit it with the greatest delight, and thank its citizens for their kind regards.

After this, John Brown Cutting, Esq. at the request of the committee of arrangements, and in behalf of himself and other revolutionary officers, delivered a short address and complimentary poem, in a handsome and appropriate manner.

After having made a reply to this address, the General was introduced to some other gentlemen; and was then conducted by the Mayor, attended by the committee of arrangements, in the way by which he had ascended, to the front door of the north wing of the Capitol, where the military passed in review before him, saluting as they passed. Immediately after his reception in the portico, a grand salute was fired in the neighborhood of the Capitol by a company of Alexandria artillery. The review being finished, the Mayor ascended the landau with the General, attended by Gen. Brown and Com. Tingey, and the procession was resumed in the same order as before; and passing through Pennsylvania Avenue, proceeded to the President's house. In this passage the streets were lined with spectators; but the most pleasing sight was the windows on each side of it filled with ladies, in their best attire and looks, bestowing, with beaming eyes, their benedictions on the beloved Chief, and waving white handkerchiefs, as tokens of their happiness.

On passing the centre market, another salute was fired from a battery south of the Tiber, by a company of artillery.

The General, with his son, the Mayor, committee of arrangements, &c. thus escorted, having reached the President's house, (distant from the Capitol more than a mile) passed into the gate of the enclosure, and thence to the portico of the mansion. The General, on alighting, was there received by the Marshal of the District of Columbia, and, supported by Gen. Brown and Com. Tingey, and accompanied by the Mayor and others of the committee of arrangements, was, with his son conducted into the drawing room where the President was prepared to receive him.

The President, stationed at the head of this circular apartment, had on his right hand the Secretary of State and the Secretary of the Treasury, on his left the Secretary of War and the Secretary of the Navy, and, ranged on each side the room, were the other gentlemen invited to be present at this interview. The whole number of distinguished persons present being fifty or sixty.

On the General's reaching the centre of the circle, the President advanced to him, and gave him a cordial and affectionate reception, such as might have been expected from the illustrious representative of the American people, to one of those early friends of theirs, whom, like himself, they delight to honor.

After the interchange of courtesies between the guest and the President, he was welcomed by the Heads of Departments. Between him and Mr. Crawford, with whom he had in France an intimate acquaintance, the meeting was that of old and affectionate friends: and by all he was respectfully and kindly greeted. Subsequently, the General was introduced in succession, by the Chief of each Department of the Government, to the officers attached to each. Liberal refreshments were then offered to the company, and fifteen or twenty minutes were spent in delightful conversation. After which the General took his leave, well pleased with his reception, and, remounting the landau, proceeded to rejoin his escort.

Retiring from this affecting scene, the General passed in review, and was saluted by the whole body of troops, which had been wheeled into line, and extended from the President's square to the General's quarters. On his alighting, he expressed his thanks to them for the honor bestowed on him, and then another grand salute was fired by a company of artillery: after which, the military were dismissed. He retired, for a short time, to his private room; and, when he returned into public, was, with his suite; introduced to a great number of citizens, anxious to express their heartfelt respect to the disinterested champion of their country's liberty.

To an address from the Mayor, full of fine feeling, the General made the following reply:—

"The kind and flattering reception with which I am honored by the citizens of Washington, excite the most lively feelings of gratitude; those grateful feelings, sir, at every step of my happy visit to the United States, could not but enhance the inexpressible delight I have enjoyed at the sight of the immense and wonderful improvements, so far beyond even the fondest anticipations of a warm American heart; and which, in the space of forty years, have so gloriously evinced the superiority of popular institutions, and self government, over the too imperfect state of political civilization, found in every part of the other hemisphere. In this august place, which bears the most venerable of all ancient and modern names, I have, sir, the pleasure to contemplate, not only a centre of that constitutional Union so necessary to these States, so important to the interests of mankind; but also a great political school, where attentive observers from other parts of the world may be taught the practical science of true social order.

"Among the circumstances of my life, to which you have been pleased to allude, none can afford me such dear recollections, as my having been early adopted as an American soldier; so there is not a circumstance of my reception in which I take so much pride, as in sharing those honors with my beloved companions in arms. Happy I am to feel that the marks of affection and esteem bestowed on me, bear testimony to my perseverance in the American principles I received under the tent of Washington, and of which I shall, to my last breath, prove myself a devoted disciple. I beg you, Mr. Mayor, and the gentlemen of the Corporation, to accept my respectful acknowledgments to you and to the citizens of Washington."

To the address and poem presented by John Brown Cutting, Esq. the General made the following reply: —

"While I embrace you, sir, and make my acknowledgments to those of our revolutionary comrades, in whose name you welcome me to this metropolis, be assured that I reciprocate those kind expressions of attachment, which from them are peculiarly gratifying. And although, in doing this, it cannot be expected that I should command such beautiful language as you employ, yet I speak from the bottom of my heart, when I assure you that the associations of time and place, to which you allude, exalt the interest which I shall ever feel in your prosperity, and that of every meritorious individual who belonged to the revolutionary army of the United States."

After the ceremony of the procession, &c. a public dinner was provided, at which the Mayor of Washington presided, assisted by the Presidents of the boards of Aldermen and the Common Council; and at which were present, the heads of departments, revolutionary officers, military and naval officers of the United States, members of the City Council, and many distinguished characters from different parts of the nation.

His reception by Mr. Monroe President of the United States, was most cordial and honorable. He called on the President, the day of his arrival in Washington, as before mentioned. The next day he was with Mr. Monroe both at breakfast and dinner, and on Thursday, the President gave a public dinner in honor of Lafayette, at which were present, the Heads of Departments, many distinguished public characters from various parts of the Unified States, and the principal officers of the army and navy. While in Washington, he also visited the Secretaries of State, of the Treasury, and of War, and Major General Brown, of the United States army.

Gen. Lafayette rode over to Georgetown, on Thursday, having been earnestly invited by the Mayor and corporation to visit the city. And the citizens demonstrated their gratitude and joy on the occasion, by a military escort, and a respectable precession. But the most acceptable offering was such as he had received in all other places, the spontaneous and cordial salutations of the whole people. On Friday, he visited the navy yard, by invitation of the veteran Commodore Tingey. His reception here was remarkably brilliant and impressive; he was accompanied by many distinguished citizens and public functionaries; and the attentions of the naval veteran were honorable to himself and highly gratifying to General Lafayette. He dined again, this day (Friday) with President Monroe; and on Saturday proceeded on his proposed visit to Alexandria, and Yorktown. He was accompanied as far as the Potomac by the Mayor and committee of arrangements from Washington, escorted by the Georgetown cavalry. On the south side of the river, he was received by the deputation of Alexandria, attended by many other citizens, and several officers of the army and navy of the United States. He was received in Alexandria with the highest military honors, and escorted through the town amidst the welcomes and shouts of many thousands of inhabitants. A public dinner was given him; and the highest regard manifested by all classes of people for this disinterested friend of American freedom and independence.

Sunday morning he visited the tomb of Washington, at Mount Vernon, accompanied by Mr. Custis, the nearest male relative of that most distinguished patriot. Lafayette spent an hour at this hallowed spot, where, were deposited the mortal remains of his most respected friend, whom he loved, venerated and was ever desirous to imitate. It was a moment of sacred recollection; and while the living patriot and hero reflected with mingled emotions of joy and sadness at the grave of one who was his leader and examplar, in youth, he could not but anticipate, with deep solemnity, the approaching period of his own departure. Mr. Custis here presented him with a ring containing some of the hair of his immortal relative. General Lafayette then proceeded on his way to Yorktown, where he arrived on Monday; and was received with great demonstrations of respect and joy. A steamboat was dispatched from Yorktown down the river to meet the United States steam boat, which had Lafayette on board. He entered the former near the mouth of the river, where he was received by the committee from Yorktown, and conveyed to that place, attended by four other large boats, crowded with citizens anxious to see and welcome "the guest of the nation." One of the committee addressed him, in a very affectionate and impressive manner, as soon as he came on board of the Virginia steamboat. A great concourse of people from the neighbouring towns were collected, and many from far distant places, together with the most distinguished public characters in the whole state of Virginia. There were also present on this occasion, many officers of high rank of the army and navy of the United States.

Great preparations had been made by the citizens of Virginia, and by the state authorities, to celebrate the anniversary of the capture of the British army, under Lord Cornwallis, at this place, on the 19th of October, 1781; an event, in which Lafayette took a very active and useful part; perhaps no general in the siege, under Washington, was more active and useful—an event, also, which had great and immediate influence with the English government, to acknowledge our independence and offer terms of an honorable peace. General Lafayette had been invited, some weeks before, to be present in Yorktown, at this time. The Ex-Presidents Jefferson and Madison, were also invited to attend, but they both declined. Mr. Madison's want of health prevented; and Mr. Jefferson declined on account of age and infirmity. We give his letter in reply to the invitation.

"Monticello, Oct. 9, 1824.

"SIR,

"I received, on the 2d instant, your favor of September 27, conveying to me the obliging invitation of the volunteer companies of the state, to meet them and their distinguished guest; Gen. Lafayette, at York on the 19th instant. No person rejoices more than I do at the effusions of gratitude with which our fellow-citizens, in all parts, are receiving this their antient and virtuous friend and benefactor; nor can any other more cordially participate in their sentiments of affection to him. Age and infirmities, however, disable me from repairing to distant occasions of joining personally in these celebrations; and leave me to avail myself of the opportunity which the friendship of the General will give by his kind assurance of a visit. He will here have the pleasure of reviewing a scene which his military maneuvers covered from the robberies and ravages of an unsparing enemy. Here, then, I shall have the welcome opportunity of joining with my grateful neighbors in manifestations of our sense of his protection peculiarly afforded to us and claiming our special remembrance and acknowledgements. But I shall not the less participate with my distant brethren by sincerely sympathising in their warmest expressions of gratitude and respect to their country's guest.

"With this apology for my inability to profit of the honorable invitation of the volunteer companies, I pray you to accept for them and yourself the assurance of my high respect and consideration.

Hon. Mr. Marshall, the Chief Justice of the United States, Major-General Taylor of the Virginia militia, Mr. Bassett, many years a member of Congress from the state, and a committee from York-town, went in the steamboat to meet General Lafayette. The address of one of the committee, on his entering the Virginia steamboat, was as follows:

"We are deputed by our fellow citizens now assembled at York-town, to welcome you to Virginia.

"We will not recount, in your presence, the real services you have rendered this republic, and the virtues that so endear you to us, lest even the simple voice of truth might pain the delicacy of a mind like yours. But the emotions we all feel, of gratitude, affection and veneration for you; emotions rendered more intense in each, by the universal sympathy of others; these we cannot suppress. In the numerous assembly, now anxiously awaiting your arrival, they are swelling in every bosom, and hanging on every tongue, and beaming from every eye.

"Yes, sir, you "read your history in a nation's eyes." A whole people unite in one deep and glowing sentiment of respect and love towards you. Wheresoever you go, the old greet you as their leader in arms, and their companion in toil and danger; the partaker, too, of their triumph. The young have been taught, from their earliest childhood, to honor and to bless your name. The mothers and the daughters of the land shed tears of joy at your approach. Your name is associated in the memory of us all, with every name, and wish most of the events in our annals, dearest to the American heart; with the illustrious and revered name of Washington, and with the most glorious achievements of the revolution.

"But, of all the states in the Union—though we will not say that Virginia is the most grateful—yet she certainly owes you the largest debt of gratitude. This state was the chief scene of your services. In the day of her greatest peril, in the darkest hour of her distress, when invading armies threatened to overrun the country, and all the horrors of war were pointed against our very dwellings; Washington selected you, his youthful friend, for the chief command, and securely entrusted the defence of his native state to your courage and conduct. How zealously you undertook, how well you fulfilled the arduous part assigned you, with what honor to yourself, and with what advantage to us, no time shall obliterate the remembrance. The general of the enemy, in effect, pronounced your eulogium, when conscious of his own abilities, and confiding in the superiority of his forces, he vauntingly said, "The boy cannot escape me." History records, not only that our youthful general did escape him, but that he held safe the far greater part of the country, in spite of his utmost efforts; and came at last to yonder spot, to assist in the capture of his army; to witness the downfall of his hopes, the humiliation of his pride, and the last effort of British power against American freedom. And now, after the lapse of forty-three years, he visits the name spot again—happy to renew there the glorious recollections of the past; and yet, happier, we hope, to see how dearly we appreciate the blessings of liberty and independence which he assisted us to achieve.

"On that spot, sir, we are most proud to receive you. We hail you as the hero of liberty and the friend of man. We greet you as the bosom friend of Washington. We greet you as one of the father's of the republic."

General Lafayette answered—

"I am happy, sir, to find myself again, after a long absence, and to be so kindly welcomed, on the beloved sail of the state of Virginia; that state, to which I am bound by so many old ties of gratitude, devotion, and mutual confidence. It is to the patriotic support I found in the civil authorities of this state, whose generous spirit had already shone from the beginning of the revolutionary contest; it is to the zeal, the courage, the perseverance of the Virginia militia, in conjunction with our small gallant continental army, that we have been indebted for the success of a campaign arduous in its beginning, fruitful in its happy issue. Nothing can be more gratifying to my feelings, than the testimonies I receive of my living still in the hearts of the Virginians; and I beg you, sir, to be pleased to accept, and transmit to the citizens of this state, the cordial tribute of my grateful, constant and affectionate respect."

The beach and the heights of Yorktown were filled with anxious spectators: the anticipation was intense. The Governor and Council were stationed on a temporary wharf, erected for the occasion, to receive him. Judges, revolutionary patriots, officers of the army, invited guests and citizens, were also in waiting, in a separate group. Lafayette landed with his companions, and supported by Colonels Fassett, Harvie, Peyton and Jones; who introduced him to the Governor of the State. The latter received him with the following speech: —

"GENERAL LAFAYETTE,

"SIR — On behalf of the people of Virginia, I tender to you a most cordial and hearty welcome to our State.

"In you we recognise the early, the steadfast, the consistent friend. Whilst the United States in general, owe you so large a debt of gratitude, for the liberal tender of your purse, your person and your blood in their behalf, the state of Virginia, is, if possible, still more deeply indebted to you. — You were her defender in the hour of her greatest trial. At the early age of twenty four years, with an army greatly inferior in numbers, and still more in equipments and discipline, you conducted your military movements with so much judgment, that the ablest officer of the British army could never obtain the slightest advantage over you; and whilst that officer spent his time in harassing our distressed state you maneuvered before him with the most unceasing caution and vigilance, with a steady eye, to that grand result, which brought the war to a crisis on the plains of York.

"Forty-three years from that period, we have the happiness to find you in our country, the vast improvement of which is the most conclusive evidence of the correctness of the principles for which you contended by the side of Washington.

"I will conclude, sir, by the expression of a sentiment, which I believe to be strictly true; It is, that no man, at any time has ever received the effusions of a nation's feelings, which have come so directly from the heart."

The General advanced, and grasping the Governor's hand, said,—"I am gratified sir, most highly gratified, by the reception you have given me on the part of the state of Virginia. The happy conduct and the successful termination of the decisive campaign, in which you have the goodness to ascribe to me so large a part, were attributable much more to the constituted authorities and people of Virginia, than to the general who was honored with the chief military command. I have the liveliest recollection of all the scenes of my services in this state, and of all the men with whom it was my happiness and honor to serve—and happy as I was to assist and witness the accomplishment of American liberty and independence, I have been yet happier in the assurance that the blessings which have flowed from that great event, have exceeded the fondest and most sanguine expectations."

The General was then successively introduced to the councilors, the judges, the revolutionary officers, and a number of citizens. The procession then advanced—Gen. Lafayette, the Governor, Chief Justice, and Mr. Calhoun, the Secretary of War, seated in the barouche. Next Lafayette's son and suite, and the Council, &c. &c. in regular succession. It advanced (the General's head uncovered) amidst the salutes from the artillery company stationed on the heights and from the steamboats and small craft—and amid the full swell of music. It passed through the long lines of citizens and old revolutionary soldiers arranged in two columns. It wound up the hill; and finally terminated at the General's quarters.—On entering the house (Gen. Nelson's) he was cheered by a crowd of citizens.

The introduction of a number of ladies and citizens followed—receiving all with interest and the quiet dignity of a spirit at peace within itself, and pleased with all the world. The most interesting of these interviews were with the soldiers of the revolution. One of them advanced, seized the General by the hand, exclaiming, "I was with you at Yorktown. I entered yonder redoubt at your side. I too was at the side of the gallant De Kalb, your associate in arms, when he fell in the field." The tears streamed from the veteran's eyes; and

Lafayette showed by his countenance the sympathy he felt. "Yes, my brave soldier, I am happy to have lived, to meet you once more."

After a short time, Lafayette, respecting that inestimable spirit of equality which pervades over free institutions, went forth to salute the crowd of citizens who stood in the street. He was stationed at the gate, and the long line of gratified spectators passed by him. Each person seized his hand as he passed him. To all Lafayette extended some mark of kindness and consideration. The spectacle was deeply impressive. The variety of manners in the different spectators was singularly striking. Some as they approached, fixed their eyes on his face, and lingered after they had passed, as if to drink in the last expression of its countenance. Others advanced with the deepest feelings of awe, with their eyes cast upon the earth.

On Monday, Lafayette dined with a select company of some 20 or 30, consisting of the revolutionary officers, &c. At night, some transparencies were exhibited over the door of his house, and under the Richmond marquee."

In truth, the scene exceeded all rational expectation: The committee of arrangements deserve much encomium for their enterprising spirit and judicious efforts. It is a seem which no man who saw it will ever forget. The Virginians appeared in their true colours. — The moral effects of this spectacle were sublime. There was an effect in it, which no words can describe, "tears streamed from an hundred eyes. The sentiments it diffused through several thousands of spectators, were of the loftiest character.

On this day, Monday 18th, the reception was purely civic, not a soldier appeared under arms. But on the 19th the military spectacle was imposing and brilliant. Soon after breakfast, Lafayette walked from his quarters, to the tent of Washington, surrounded by the committee of arrangements and others. Numbers were then introduced to him — many ladies, the veteran soldiers of the revolution, citizens from other states and all quarters of Virginia.

Col. Wm. I. Lewis, of Campbell, was introduced to him, and delivered the following address: —

"GEN. LAFAYETTE,

"The sons of the mountains join most cordially their low land brethren in welcoming your return to this country, they are the more delighted at this particular period, because after an absence of about forty years, you will now be a witness of the happy effects of self government, founded on the natural rights of man—rights, which you so nobly contributed to establish. Little did you think when in youthful age, you voluntarily put your life in your hand, and crossed the stormy billows of the deep, to fight and bleed for the independence of America that the results would have been so wonderful. At that period we were only a handful of people, for in everything of military import, except an invincible love and attachment for liberty—we fought, and thanks to Lafayette and his native nation, we conquered!—Now we see the result—we have nearly by the offspring of our own loins increased to more than 10,000,000 of people cleared the immeasurable forests of savages, and wild beasts, and in their places are cultivating rich fields, building villages, towns, and cities; our commerce is spread over every sea, and our navy rides triumphant on the ocean. Such are the effects of free government, founded on equal rights, supported by wise and merciful laws faithfully executed!—There is but one alloy to our pleasure of meeting you—we dread your return to Europe. The despots of that country envy your increasing glory, founded on virtue, which they cannot imitate; and their political fears may again incarcerate you in the grated walls of a dungeon! Stay then with us, Lafayette—stay with us—here in every house you will find a home and in every heart a friend—we will with filial affection rock with gentleness the cradle of your declining age; and when it shall please the God of universal nature to call you to himself, crowned with the blessings of at least one free and mighty nation, we will then with holy devotion bury your bones by the side of your adopted and immortal father, and moisten your tomb with the tears of love and gratitude."

The costume and whole appearance of Col. Lewis were striking and interesting; he had on the mountain dress. On the conclusion of the address, the General grasped him with both hands, and in the most touching manner, begged him to convey to his mountain friends his, most affectionate acknowledgments for this testimony of their kindness. He recounted the services which their gallantry had formerly rendered him. He dwelt with delight upon the interest they now manifested in his happiness.

About 11 o'clock, the procession began to form for the triumphal arch, erected on the ruins of the Rock Redoubt, standing within six yards of the river's bank. The ceremony of the reception at that most interesting point, was pathetic beyond expression. The old General advanced up the hillock which leads to the redoubt, limping and supported by the Governor, with his aids and members of the committee of arrangement. A large column of officers and citizens followed them. When Lafayette had reached the triumphal arch, General Taylor stepped from the semicircular group, which was formed near the river's bank, saluted him with profound respect, and addressed him in the following manner:

"GENERAL,

"On behalf of my comrades, I bid you welcome. They come to greet you, with no pageantry, intended to surprise by its novelty, or dazzle by its splendour: But they bring you. General, an offering which wealth could not purchase, nor power constrain. On this day, associated with so many thrilling recollections; on this spot, consecrated by successful valour, they come to offer you this willing homage of their hearts.

"Judge, General, of their feelings at this moment by your own. Every thing around them speaks alike to their senses and sensibilities. These plains, where the peaceful plow-share has not yet effaced the traces of military operations; these half decayed ramparts, this ruined village, in which the bombs' havoc is still every where visible, tell us of past warfare; and remind us of that long, arduous and doubtful struggle, on the issue of which depended the emancipation of our country.

"On yonder hillock, the last scene of blood was closed by the surrender of an army; and the liberty of our nation permanently secured. With what resistless eloquence does it persuade our gratitude and admiration for the gallant heroes, to whose noble exertions we owe the countless blessings which our free institutions have conferred upon us?

"The spot on which we stand was once a redoubt occupied by our enemy. With how rapid a pencil does imagination present the blooming chieftain, by whom it was wrested from his grasp. Can we be here and forget, that superior to the prejudices which then enchained even noble minds, he perceived in the first and almost hopeless struggles of a distant and obscure colony, the movement of that moral power, which was destined to give an new direction and character to political institutions, and to improve human happiness. Can we forget, that, deaf to the solicitations of power, of rank, and of pleasure, with a noble prodigality, he gave to our country his sword, his treasure, and the influence of his example.

"And when in the aged warrior who stands before us, we recognise that youthful chieftain, with what rapidity does memory retrace the incidents of his eventful life? With what pleasure do we see his manhood realize the promise of his youth? In senates or in camps, in the palaces of kings, or in their *dungeons*, we behold the same erect and manly spirit. At one time tempering the licentiousness of popular feeling; at another restraining the extravagance of power, and always regardless of every thing but the great object of his life, the moral and political improvement of mankind.

"General — In the brightest days of antiquity, no artificial stimulus of rank or power, or wealth, was required to excite noble minds to acts of generous daring, A wreath of laurel, or of oak, was at once the proof and the reward of illustrious merit. For this, statesmen meditated, warriors bled, and eloquence soared to its sublimest heights. The prize was invaluable; for, it was won only by merit. It detracted, however, somewhat from its worth, that it was conferred by the partiality of compatriots, and in the fervor of admiration inspired by recent success.

"Your life, General, illustrious throughout, in this also is distinguished. — Time which dims the lustre of ordinary merit, has rendered yours more brilliant. After a lapse of nearly half a century, your triumph is decreed by the sons of those who witnessed your exploits.

"Deign then, General, to accept the simple but expressive token of their gratitude and admiration. Suffer their leader to place upon your veteran brow the only crown it would not disdain to wear, the blended emblems of civic worth and martial prowess. It will not pain you, General, to perceive some scattered sprigs of melancholy cypress intermingled with the blended leaves of laurel and oak. Your heart would turn from us with generous indignation, if on an occasion like this, amid the joyous acclamations which greet you, every where, were heard no sighs of grateful recollection for those gallant men who shared your battles, but do not, cannot share your triumph. The wreath which our gratitude has woven to testify our love for you, will lose nothing of its fragrance, or its verdure, though time hang upon its leaves some tears of pious recollection of the friend of your early youth; In war the avenger, in peace, the father of his country.

"In behalf then, of all the chivalry of Virginia; on this redoubt which his valour wrested from the enemy at the point of the bayonet; I place on the head of Major General Lafayette this wreathe of double triumph:—won by numerous and illustrious acts of martial prowess, and by a life devoted to the happiness of the human race. In their names, I proclaim him alike victorious in arms and acts of civil polity. In bannered fields, a hero—in civil life, the benefactor of mankind."

Lafayette was deeply affected. There was a solemn earnestness in his manner, a touching sensibility in his whole countenance which most deeply impressed every observer. Many wept—all were moved. When Gen. Taylor had closed his address, he was about to fix the civic wreath upon the General's head. But the considerate veteran, always himself, always attentive to the slightest proprieties of word and action, caught the hovering wreath as it approached his brow with his right hand, and respectfully bowing, dropt it to his side, when he thus replied:

"I most cordially thank you, my dear general, and your companions in arms, for your affectionate welcome, your kind recollections, and the flattering expressions of your friendship. Happy I am to receive them on these already ancient lines, where the united arms of America and France have been gloriously engaged in a holy alliance to support the rights of American Independence, and he sacred principle of the sovereignty of the people. Happy also to be so welcomed on the particular spot where my dear light infantry comrades acquired one of their honorable claims to public love and esteem. You know, sir, that in this business of storming redoubts, with unloaded arms and fixed bayonets, the merit of the deed is in the soldiers who execute it, and to each of them, I am anxious to acknowledge their equal share of honor. Let me, however, with affection and gratitude, pay a special tribute to the gallant name of Hamilton, who commanded the attack, to the three field officers who seconded him, Gimat, Laurens and Fish, the only surviving one, my friend now near me. In their name, my dear general, in the name of the light infantry, those we have lost as well as those who survive, and only in common with them, I accept the crown with which you are pleased to honor us, and I offer you the return of the most grateful acknowledgements."

When he had closed, he gave a new proof of the rapidity of his conceptions, the generosity of his soul, the uniform modesty of his character. The very moment he concluded, (never having been prepared for such a scene, never having seen the address, never having suspected the presentation of the wreath) he turned round and drew Col. Fish to the front. "Here," he exclaimed, "half of this wreath belongs to you." "No sir, it is all your own." "Then" said Lafayette, putting it into Col. Fish's hand, "take it and preserve it as our *common property.*"

The whole scene was strongly marked by the moral sublime. This ceremony over, the grand review commenced. Lafayette stood near the arch, and the volunteer companies, and the U. S. troops passed him in regular succession, with flags flying and music floating in the air. The troops then formed themselves again in line, and Lafayette on foot, passed down the line. He was carried to the obelisk, situated on the spot where Vimionel had stormed the second redoubt. — The review over, and Lafayette having seen and been seen by all the troops, be mounted his barouche in company with the governor, and was followed by the other carriages. The whole body of military and citizens then moved to the field, near to which the British troops had grounded their arms in 1781. Between these, and the amphitheatre, where at least one thousand ladies sat, the barouche passed on near to the ladies, who continued to wave their white handkerchiefs as he slowly moved on. "Ladies, receive my warm thanks for your kind welcome," was constantly upon his lips.

The whole scene defies description. Here were the fields, which forty-three years ago, had witnessed the tread of a conquered enemy! A thousand associations of this description rushed upon the mind. Now, filled with an animated and joyous throng of from 10 to 15,000 persons. The spectacle surpassed all expectation; all expression.

When at the tomb of Washington, Mr. Custis addressed him as follows: —

"Last of the generals of the army of Independence! At this awful and impressive moment, when forgetting the splendour of a triumph greater than Roman consul ever had, you bend with reverence over the remains of Washington, the child of Mount Vernon presents you with this token, containing the hair of him, whom while living you loved, and to whose honored grave you now pay the manly and affecting tribute of a patriot's and a soldier's tear.

"The *ring* has ever been an emblem of the union of hearts from the earliest ages of the world; and *this* will unite the affections of all the Americans to the person and posterity of Lafayette, now and hereafter. And when your descendants of a distant day shall behold this valued relic, it will remind them of the heroic virtues of their illustrious sire, who received it, not in the palaces of princes, or amid the pomp and vanities of life, but at the laurelled grave of Washington.

"Do you ask — Is this the Mausoleum befitting the ashes of a Marcus Aurelius, or the good Antonius? I tell you, that the father of his country lies buried in the hearts of his countrymen; and in those of the brave, the good, the free, of all ages and nations. Do you seek for the tablets, which are to convey his fame to immortality? They have long been written in the freedom and happiness of their country. These are the monumental trophies of Washington the great; and will endure when the proudest works of art have "dissolved and left not a wreck behind."

"Venerable man! will you never tire in the cause of freedom and human happiness? Is it not time that you should rest from your labours, and repose on the bosom of a country, which delights to love and honor you, and will teach her children's children to bless your name and memory? Surely, where liberty dwells, there must be the country of Lafayette.

"Our fathers witnessed the dawn of your glory, partook of its meridian splendour; and oh, let their children enjoy the benign radiance of your setting sun. And when it shall sink in the horizon of nature, here, here with pious duty, we will form your sepulcher; and, united in death as in life, by the side of the great chief you will rest in peace, till the last trump awakes the slumbering world, and call your virtues to their great reward.

"The joyous shouts of millions of freemen hailed your returning foot-print on our sands. The arms of millions are opened wide to take you to their grateful hearts, and the prayers of millions ascend to the throne of the Eternal, that the choicest blessings of heaven may cheer the latest days of Lafayette."

General Lafayette having received the ring, pressed it to his bosom, and replied—

"The feelings, which at this awful moment oppress my heart, do not leave the power of utterance I can only thank you, my dear Custis, for your precious gift. I pay a silent homage to the tomb of the greatest and best of men, my paternal friend."

General Lafayette was escorted to his quarters by the troops, and a sumptuous dinner provided for him, and the distinguished civil and military characters who were present on the occasion. The following morning, the officers of the volunteer companies present, prepared a military breakfast. The table was spread in the tent of Washington, which was pitched at the volunteer's encampment. He left York Wednesday afternoon, and reached Williamsburg in the evening, where he was received with open arms by the citizens. Hence he proceeded to Norfolk, where he had been previously invited, and where great preparations were made to receive him according to his distinguished merit, and his highly important services to the country. From Norfolk he was to proceed to Richmond; and thence farther south through North and South Carolina, to Georgia. Invitations have been given him to visit Kentucky, Tennessee and Ohio; but it is probable he will decline them. For he intends returning to Washington in December, and to spend most of the winter season in that city. Early in the spring, he will probably visit the northern states again; and embark for France at Boston, some time in June or July.

There is a strong and very general desire that Lafayette should pass the remainder of his life in the United States; and that the national government should provide a respectable establishment for him and his family in this country. That the representatives of the people will be ready to grant an honorable stipend, there cannot be a doubt. But France is his native country and his home. There are his children and his grand children. There, it is natural, he should desire to pass his few remaining years. And such an intention, we believe, he has expressed. What will be his final resolution on the subject, we will not conjecture.

* * * * *

From the New-York Commercial Advertiser.

LAFAYETTE.

O deep was the gloom on our sad land descending,
  And wild was the moan from the tempest's dread form,
While the heroes and sires of our country were bending
  Their souls to their God, and their brows to the storm.

Who bounds to the shore from the dark bosom'd ocean,
  In the sparkle and pride of his beauty and youth?
His ardent mind burning, his soul all devotion,
  To the high cause of liberty, justice and truth?

He joins the bold band, who, with spirits undaunted,
  Strive to guard and to win, all man's bosom holds dear;
It is done! they have triumph'd! and heaven has granted

Fair freedom to crown their majestic career.

How lovely the land where the bright sun is flinging
  The purple and gold from his throne in the west!
There millions of hearts in their gladness are singing,
  There finds the poor exile contentment and rest.

The eagle that rush'd on a torn, bloody pinion,
  And soar'd to the sky 'mid the clamors of light,
Now wings his proud way in untroubled dominion,
  While the nations all silently gaze on his flight.

Who comes o'er the billow with head bent and hoary,
  With full throbbing heart, and with glistening eye
Past years roll before him — the scene of his glory
  Fills his heart with emotions, deep, solemn and high.

Great man! thy lov'd name to the skies is ascending,
  A name whose remembrance no time can destroy,
While gladness and grief are within us contending,
  For all *thou* hast suffer'd, and all *we* enjoy.

We will rank thee with him, who was sent us by heaven;
  Ye shall meet in our hearts as in glory ye met:
Spread, ye winds, the glad news! to our wishes is given
  The friend of our WASHINGTON, brave LAFAYETTE.

* * * * *

TO LAFAYETTE.

We'll search the earth, and search the sea,
To cull a gallant wreath for thee;
And every field for freedom fought,
And every mountain-height, where aught
Of liberty can yet be found,

Shall be our blooming harvest-ground.

Laurels in garlands hang upon
Thermopylae and Marathon;—
On Bannockburn the thistle grows;—
On Runnymead the wild rose blows;—
And on the banks of Boyne, its leaves
Green Erin's shamrock wildly weaves.
In France, in sunny France, we'll get
The Fleur-de-lys and mignonette
From every consecrated spot,
Where ties a martyr'd Huguenot;—.
And cull *even here*, from many a field,
And many a rocky height,
Bays, that our vales and mountains yield,
Where men have met to fight
For law, and liberty, and life,
And died in freedom's holy strife.
Below Atlantic seas,—below
The waves of Erie and Champlain,
The sea-grass and the corals grow
In rostral trophies round the slain;
And we can add to form thy crown,
Some branches worthy thy renown.
Long may the chaplet flourish bright,
And borrow from the heavens its light!
As with a cloud that circles round
A star, when other stars are set,
With glory shall thy brow be bound,
With glory shall thy head be crowned,
With glory-starlike tinctured yet:—
For air, and earth, and, sky, and sea,
Shall yield a glorious wreath to thee